BIGGEST
RIDDLE
BOOK
IN THE
WORLD

by Joseph Rosenbloom

illustrated by
Joyce Behr

 Sterling Publishing Co., Inc.   New York

Books by Joseph Rosenbloom

Biggest Riddle Book in the World
Doctor Knock-Knock's Offical Knock-Knock
    Dictionary
Funny Insults & Snappy Put-Downs
Gigantic Joke Book
The Little Giant Book of Riddles
The Little Giant Book of Jokes
Zaniest Riddle Book in the World

To: Michelle, Michael and Eric

Revised Edition

10 9 8 7 6 5 4 3

Published by Sterling Publishing Company, Inc.
387 Park Avenue South, New York, N.Y. 10016
© 1976 by Joseph Rosenbloom
Distributed in Canada by Sterling Publishing
℅ Canadian Manda Group, One Atlantic Avenue, Suite 105
Toronto, Ontario, Canada M6K 3E7
Distributed in Great Britain and Europe by Cassell PLC
Wellington House, 125 Strand, London WC2R 0BB, England
Distributed in Australia by Capricorn Link (Australia) Pty Ltd.
P.O. Box 6651, Baulkham Hills, Business Centre, NSW 2153, Australia
Manufactured in the United States of America
All rights reserved

Sterling ISBN 0-8069-8884-3

Contents

Introduction

This book grew out of my many years experience as a professional librarian working with children.

"Where are the riddle books?" and "Do you have any more riddle books?" were two questions frequently asked by many young readers. And once through a riddle book or two, the reader was ready to search out a likely victim on whom his repertoire could be practiced. A receptive librarian was as good as any for this purpose. The children soon discovered that I could be relied on to listen to anyone who had a riddle to tell. Their pleasure in riddles proved contagious. Soon, I became addicted to telling riddles of my own. Our exchange of riddles back and forth over the years resulted in a substantial collection which forms the core of this book.

Why do children enjoy riddles so immensely? First, riddles are based on language and logic. To tell a riddle, all you need do is communicate with someone capable of understanding what you are saying. There are no rules to riddles—and you don't need any equipment either. Second, languages, English, in particular, have a large number of words with more than one meaning. These words provide a vast reservoir of material from which riddles may be developed. For example:

Question: How can a leopard change his spots?

Answer: *Move to another place.*

This riddle depends on the double meaning of "spot" as both a mark on a leopard's coat and as a physical location.

Another rich source of riddle fun comes from the fact that the expected or reasonable answer turns out to be the wrong one. For example:

Question: Why do surgeons wear masks during operations?

Answer: *Because if they make a mistake, no one will know who did it.*

The reasonable explanation—that surgeons wear masks for purposes of medical hygiene—is replaced by a ridiculous answer, that they want to hide their identity in the event they slip up.

No punishment awaits failure to answer the riddles we ask each other. The inability to answer them correctly has no real or serious consequences. But much of the fun is in the asking—riddles are not really intended to be solitary affairs.

Enjoying riddles usually begins around second grade or at about seven years of age, when riddles quickly become children's favorite form of verbal play. Just as physical play helps to develop the young body for adult life, verbal play helps sharpen young minds. Often riddles teach the children something they did not know before about words or about logical relationships. When this happens, the riddle becomes a learning experience.

This collection is intended to provide a rich source of riddles for children of any age or stage of intellectual attainment. There are simple riddles and complex ones, outright gags and mental puzzlers, puns and conundrums, classic riddles and contemporary ones. My object was to furnish a single giant riddle book which will serve the child from his earliest interest in riddles right on through adulthood. The scope and variety of the riddles in the collection will, I hope, not only provide endless hours of amusement, but also help to stimulate intellectual growth.

1 Warm Ups

What happens when you throw a green rock in the Red Sea?
It gets wet.

What does an envelope say when you lick it?
Nothing. It just shuts up.

Why shouldn't you tell a secret to a pig?
Because he is a squealer.

Where do frogs sit?
On toadstools.

Why should you leave your watch home when you take an airplane?
Because time flies anyway.

If a man were born in Greece, raised in Spain, came to America, and died in San Francisco, what is he?
Dead.

How can you tell twin witches apart?
It's not easy to tell which witch is which.

What weighs more: a pound of lead or a pound of feathers?

They weigh the same.

Why did the man have to fix the horn of his car?

Because it didn't give a hoot.

Why did the nutty kid throw a bucket of water out of the window?

He wanted to make a big splash.

Why did the nutty kid throw butter out of the window?

He wanted to see a butterfly.

Why did the nutty kid throw a glass of water out of the window?

He wanted to see a waterfall.

What paper makes you itch?

Scratch paper.

What can you break without touching it?
Your promise.

Why do people always say to you, "A penny for your thoughts?"
Because that's all they are worth.

A man was driving a black truck. His lights were not on. The moon was not out. A lady was crossing the street. How did the man see her?
It was a bright, sunny day.

What is a Mexican weather report?
Chili today, hot tamale.

What doesn't get any wetter no matter how much it rains?
The ocean.

What animal makes the most of its food?
The giraffe. It makes a little go a long way.

What insect gets A's in English?
A spelling bee.

When a dirty kid has finished taking a bath, what is still dirty?
The bathtub.

What kind of bath can you take without water?
A sun bath.

What time is the same spelled backward or forward?
Noon.

What do you get if you cross an insect and a rabbit?
Bugs Bunny.

Why can't you read a story about a bed?
It hasn't been made up yet.

Why did the kid avoid the cemetery?
He wouldn't be caught dead there.

If a fifty cent piece and a quarter were on the Empire State Building, which would jump off first?
The quarter, because it has less sense (cents).

What did the bee say to the flower?
"Hello, honey!"

What did the fly say to the flypaper?
"I'm stuck on you."

What did the tree say to the woodpecker?
"You bore me."

What color was Napoleon's white horse?
White.

Why did the kid put his clock in the oven.
He wanted to have a hot time.

What ten letter word starts with g-a-s?
Automobile.

If you want to get rich, why should you keep your mouth shut?

Because silence is golden.

What is drawn by everyone without pen or pencil?
Breath.

What goes around a yard but doesn't move?
A fence.

Why does a mother carry her baby?
The baby can't carry the mother.

What is a calf after it is six months old?
Seven months old.

What asks no question but demands an answer?
A doorbell or a ringing telephone.

What kind of apple has a short temper?
A crab apple.

How does a boat show affection?
It hugs the shore.

What kind of watch is best for people who don't like time on their hands?

A pocket watch.

What goes up and down but doesn't move?

A staircase.

What always comes into a house through the keyhole?

A key.

What word if pronounced right is wrong but if pronounced wrong is right?

Wrong.

What song does a car radio play?

A cartoon (car tune).

What has four legs and a back but no body?

A chair.

When does a chair dislike you?

When it can't bear you.

What kind of electricity do they have in Washington?
D.C. (Direct Current).

How did the man feel when he got a big bill from the electric company?
He was shocked.

What did the man do when he got a big gas bill?
He exploded.

What did the man say when he got a big phone bill?
"Who said talk is cheap?"

What is the best day to go to the beach?
Sunday.

What kind of bulbs don't need water?
Light bulbs.

Why is a fish like a person who talks too much?
Because it doesn't know when to keep its mouth shut.

How can you tell the difference between a can of chicken soup and a can of tomato soup?
Read the label.

What trees come in two's?
Pear (pair) trees.

What insect runs away from everything?
A flea (flee).

What kind of cup doesn't hold water?
A cupcake.

What animal doesn't believe anything?
Sheep. They always say, "Bah! Bah!"

Why did the reporter put a flashlight into his mouth?
He wanted to get the inside story.

What is the first thing you see
when you understand something?
You see the light.

Do you say, "Nine and five is
thirteen," or "Nine and five are
thirteen"?
*Neither. Nine and five are
fourteen.*

What people travel the most?
Romans.

What person is always in a hurry?
A Russian.

What does Brazil produce
that no other country
produces?
Brazilians.

What people are like the end of a book?
The Finnish.

Who never gets his hair wet in the shower?
A bald man.

Why did Jack and Jill roll down the hill?
It beats walking.

How many animals did Moses take on the ark?
Moses didn't take anything on the ark. Noah did!

What two things can't you have for breakfast?
Lunch and dinner.

What flower does everyone have?
Tulips (two lips).

What bird can lift the most?
A crane.

What belongs to you, but is used more by others?
Your name.

What did the light switch say to the girl?
"You turn me on."

What did one wall say to the other?
"I'll meet you at the corner."

What did the big chimney say to the little chimney?
"You are too young to smoke."

Why do firemen wear red suspenders?
To keep their pants up.

What is the difference between a pear and a pearl?
The letter L.

What does a caterpillar do on New Year's Day?
Turns over a new leaf.

Who can marry a lot of wives and still be single?
A minister.

Why does a pencil seem heavy when you write with it for a long time?
Because it is full of lead.

What kind of coach has no wheels?
A football coach.

How do pigs write?
With a pigpen.

Why do we buy clothes?
Because we can't get them free.

What kind of tree do you find in the kitchen?
A pantry.

Where did the knights study?
In knight (night) school.

What can run but can't walk?
Water.

What is the first thing you do in the morning?
You wake up.

What is a zebra?
A horse with venetian blinds.

Why is an engaged girl like a telephone?
Because they both have rings.

Why do postmen carry letters?
Because the letters can't go anywhere by them-selves.

What kind of hogs do you find on highways?
Road hogs.

Who always goes to bed with shoes on?
A horse.

Why is a toupee like a secret?
Because you keep it under your hat.

Spell "pound" in two letters.
Lb.

Why shouldn't you put grease on your hair the night
before a test?
If you did, everything might slip your mind.

What is the first thing you put into a room?
Your feet.

What is a sound sleeper?
Someone who snores.

If six children and two dogs were under an umbrella,
how come none of them got wet?
Because it wasn't raining.

If a boy is spanked by his mother and his father,
who hurts the most?
The boy.

What kind of star wears sunglasses?
A movie star.

What is the difference between here and there?
The letter T.

Can you read the following?
Yy u r yy u b
I c u r yy 4 me.
Too wise you are, too wise you be,
I see you are too wise for me.

What did one arithmetic book say to the other
arithmetic book?
"Boy, do I have problems!"

What has two hands but no arms?
A clock.

What piece of wood is like a king?
A ruler.

What do people make that you can't see?
Noise.

What did the boy squirrel say to the girl squirrel?
"I'm nuts about you."

What did the girl squirrel answer back?
"You're nuts so bad yourself."

What did one candle say to the other candle?
"Going out tonight?"

Why can't a mind reader read your mind?
He could—if you had one!

What kind of table has no legs?
A multiplication table.

What cap is never removed?
Your kneecap.

On what kind of ships do students study?
Scholarships.

When prices are going up, what remains stationary?
Writing paper and envelopes.

What did one car muffler say to the other car muffler?
"Am I exhausted!"

What did the big watch hand say to the little watch hand?
"Don't go away, I'll be back in an hour."

What did the father tree say to his son?
"You're a chip off the old block."

What has teeth but no mouth?
A comb or a saw.

Where can you always find money?
In the dictionary.

If cows talked all at once, what would they say?
Nothing. Cows can't talk.

2 Quickies

What kind of money do monsters use?
Weirdo (weird dough).

Why did the window pane blush?
It saw the weather-strip.

When is the moon heaviest?
When it is full.

How do you file a nail?
Under the letter N.

What is a parrot?
A wordy birdy.

What fly has laryngitis?
A horsefly (hoarse fly).

Why did the kid keep his shirt on when he took a bath?
Because the label said "Wash and Wear."

What kind of water can't freeze?
Hot water.

What did the big watch hand say to the small hand?
"Got a minute?"

What did one broom say to the other broom?
"Have you heard the latest dirt?"

What did the electric plug say to the wall?
"Socket to me!"

Why is an old car like a baby playing?
Because it goes with a rattle.

What knights rode camels?
The Arabian Nights (knights).

What is Dracula's favorite sport?
Bat-minton (badminton).

What letter is like a vegetable?
The letter P.

Why do people work as bakers?
Because they knead (need) the dough.

What is a sleeping bag?
A knapsack (nap sack).

Where do ants go when they want to eat?
To a restaur-ant.

What is the opposite of restaurant?
Workerant.

Who has friends for lunch?
A cannibal.

What time is it when a clock strikes thirteen?
Time to get it fixed.

What is the most valuable fish?
Goldfish.

What is a ghost's favorite rock?
Tombstone.

When is a man like a dog?
When he is a boxer.

What do you call a greasy chicken?
A slick chick.

What is the difference between a tickle and a wise guy?
One is fun, the other thinks he's fun.

Why did the cowboy ride his horse?
Because the horse was too heavy to carry.

Can you spell eighty in two letters?
A-T.

Why are diapers like $10 bills?
Because you have to change them.

Which end of a bus is it best to get off?
It doesn't matter. Both ends stop.

How does a fireplace feel?
Grate! (Great!)

What did Napoleon become after his 39th year?
40 years old.

What cat lives in the ocean?
An octopus.

What would you call a beautiful cat?
A glamour puss.

What is a wet cat?
A drizzle puss.

What do you get if you cross a cat with a laughing hyena?
A giggle puss.

What do you get if you feed a lemon to your cat?
A sourpuss.

What kind of lock is on a hippie's door?
A padlock.

Why did the man put a clock under his desk?
He wanted to work overtime.

What fish is a bargain?
A sailfish (sale fish).

What is a very hard subject?
The study of rocks.

Why was the boy's suit rusty?
It was guaranteed to wear like iron.

What stays hot in the refrigerator?
Mustard.

What kind of key opens a casket?
A skeleton key.

What is a broken down hot rod?
A shot rod.

Why is the moon like a dollar?
It has four quarters.

What wears shoes but has no feet?
The sidewalk.

Why are rivers lazy?
Because they never get off their beds.

Where do they put crying children?
In a bawl (ball) park.

What state has a friendly greeting for everyone?
Ohio.

When is a chair like a fabric?
When it is sat in (satin).

Why was the horse all charged up?
Because it ate haywire.

What is ice?
Skid stuff.

What sea creature can add?
An octoplus.

What is a vampire's favorite soup?
Alpha-bat (alphabet) soup.

What is bought by the yard and worn by the foot?
A carpet.

What have eyes but can't see?
Needles, storms and potatoes.

Why did the ocean roar?
Because it had crabs in its bed.

What insect can be spelled with just one letter?
Bee.

Why did Batman go to the pet shop?
To buy a Robin.

How do you make a lemon drop?
Hold it and then let go.

What gets around everywhere?
Belts.

What did the girl watch say to the boy watch?
"Keep your hands to yourself."

How does a baby ghost cry?
"Boo-hoo! Boo-hoo!"

Did you hear the story about the skunk?
Never mind, it stinks.

How can you double your money?
Look at it in a mirror.

How can you name the capital of every U.S. state in two seconds?
Washington, D.C.

Why are pants always too short?
Two feet are always sticking out.

What is the science of shopping?
Biology (buy-ology).

What is a good way to get fat?
Fry up some bacon.

What food is good for the brain?
Noodle soup.

What did Tennessee?
He saw what Arkansas.

Where do baby trees go to school?
To a tree nursery.

What has fifty heads and fifty tails?
Fifty pennies.

What kind of bird is like a letter?
A jaybird.

Why was the girl named Sugar?
Because she was so refined.

What is another name for a telephone booth?
A chatterbox.

What do you draw without a pencil or paper?
A window shade.

Why don't bananas ever get lonely?
Because they go around in bunches.

What did the chicks say to the miser?
"Cheap! Cheap!"

On what nuts can pictures hang?
Walnuts.

How does a broom act?
With sweeping gestures.

What kind of apple isn't an apple?
A pineapple.

What is the left side of an apple?
The part that you don't eat.

Why shouldn't you believe a person
in bed?
Because he is lying.

Why do mummies tell no secrets?
*Because they keep things under
wraps.*

How can you make seven even?
Take away the letter S.

What gives milk and has one horn?
A milk truck.

What kind of paper can you tear?
Terrible (tearable) paper.

What birds are always unhappy?
Bluebirds.

What are southern fathers called?
Southpaws.

What can you hold without touching it?
A conversation.

Why are most cows noisy?
Because they have horns.

What kind of animal tells little white lies?
An amphibian.

What food are you able to can?
Cannibal (cannable) food.

What question must always be answered, "Yes"?
"What does Y-E-S spell?"

Where was Solomon's temple?
On his head.

Why isn't a dime worth as much today as it used
to be?
Because the dimes (times) have changed.

What goes around in circles and makes kids happy?
A merry-go-round.

Why do you go to bed?
Because the bed will not come to you.

What kind of meat doesn't stand up?
Lean meat.

What kind of cattle laugh?
Laughingstock.

What horses keep late hours?
Nightmares.

What is a bee with a low buzz?
A mumble bee.

What pet is always found on the floor?
A carpet.

What is a sleeping bull?
A bull dozer.

3 Ask Your Friends —If You Dare!

What is a forum?
> *Two-um plus two-um.*

How do mountains hear?
> *With mountaineers.*

Spell Indian tent with two letters.
> *TP.*

What is the proverb about catching a cold?
> *"Win a flu (few), lose a flu."*

What happened to the wolf who fell into the washing machine?
> *He became a wash and werewolf.*

When is it difficult to get your watch off your wrist?
When it's ticking (sticking) there.

Why is a mouse like hay?
Because the cat'll (cattle) eat it.

Why doesn't Sweden export cattle?
Because she wants to keep her Stockholm (stock home).

What did Mason say to Dixon?
"We've got to draw the line somewhere."

How many peas are there in a pint?
There is only one P in "pint."

What happened when the Indian shot at Daniel Boone?
He had an arrow (narrow) escape.

Why is a barefoot boy like an Eskimo?
The barefoot boy wears no shoes and the Eskimo wears snowshoes.

At what time do most people go to the dentist?
At tooth-hurty (2:30).

Why is Saturday night important to Julius's girl friend?
That's when Julius Caesar (sees her).

How much is 5Q and 5Q?
"10Q."
"You're welcome."

Why did the man throw away all the new pennies he had?
Because they were a nuisance (new cents).

Can you spell soft and slow with two letters?
EZ.

What would happen if everyone in the country bought a pink car?
We would have a pink carnation (car nation).

Where do you end up if you smoke too much?
Coffin (coughin').

What is the best way to send a letter to the Easter Bunny?
By hare (air) mail.

What do you call an alligator's helper?
Gatorade.

When someone comes to your door, what is the polite thing to do?
Vitamin (invite him in).

Can you spell a composition with two letters?
SA (essay).

When is a grown man still a child?
When he is a miner (minor).

Where were the first French fries made?
In Greece (grease).

Why do ships use knots instead of miles?
To keep the sea tide (tied).

What vegetable is dangerous to have aboard ship?
A leek (leak).

What did the boy gopher say to the girl gopher?
"I gopher (go for) you."

What did the boy firefly say to the girl firefly?
"I glow for you."

What did the boy banana say to the girl banana?
"You have a lot of appeal."

How can you spell rot with two letters?
DK (decay).

If you add 2-forget and 2-forget, what do you get?
4-gotten.

What did Delaware?
She wore her New Jersey.

Why did the lady hold her ears when she passed the chickens?
Because she didn't want to hear their foul (fowl) language.

What musical instrument from Spain helps you fish?
A cast-a-net (castanet).

What is the difference between a fish and a piano?
You can't tuna fish.

If you put three ducks in a carton, what do you get?
A box of quackers.

What girl's name is like a letter?
Kay (K).

What has four wheels and flies?
A garbage truck.

When did the fly fly?
When the spider spied her.

What do you call a boy named Lee whom no one wants to talk to?
Lonely (Lone-Lee).

What did one tooth say to the other tooth?
"Thar's gold in them thar fills."

What is the first thing ghosts do when they get into a car?
They fasten their sheet (seat) belts.

A man and a dog were going down the street. The man rode, yet walked. What was the dog's name?

Yet.

Why do windows squeak when you open them?
Because they have panes (pains).

Why is a shirt with 8 buttons so interesting?
Because you fascinate (fasten 8).

When is a letter damp?
When it has postage due (dew).

Why is Ireland so rich?
Because its capital is always Dublin (doublin').

How can you prove that a horse has six legs?
A horse has four legs (forelegs) in front and two behind.

What did the jack say to the car?
"Can I give you a lift?"

What do you call your mother's other sister?
Deodorant (the other aunt).

What happens when two bullets get married?
They have a BB (baby).

Where does the sandman keep his sleeping sand?
In his knapsack (nap sack).

Where do you put letters to boys?
In a mail (male) box.

Why was the Lone Ranger poor?
Because he was always saying, "I owe (heigh-ho) Silver!"

Why are oranges like bells?
You can peel (peal) both of them.

If the ruler of Russia was called the Czar and his wife the Czarina, what were his children called?
Sardines.

Can you spell very happy with three letters?
XTC (ecstasy).

What tree is hairy?
A fir (fur) tree.

What is everyone's favorite tree?
A poplar (popular) tree.

Why did the tree need less sunshine?
Because it was sycamore (sick of more).

What musical instrument doesn't tell the truth?
A lyre (liar).

What did the kid say when he opened his piggy bank and found nothing?
O I C U R M T.

Why did the teacher give the zombie bad marks?
He was always making a ghoul (fool) of himself.

What part of a car is the laziest?
The wheels. They are always tired.

A man had two sons and named them both Ed. How come?
Two Eds (heads) are better than one.

What fur do you get from a skunk?
As fur (far) as possible.

What cat owes money?
A pussywillow (pussy will owe).

When is a green book not a green book?
When it is read (red).

What man in the Bible was the busiest doctor?

Job, because he had the most patience (patients).

How do you spell "we" with two letters without using the letters W and E?

U and I.

Where does a vampire take a bath?

In the bat-room (bathroom).

What holes are not holes?

Knotholes (not holes).

What is a panther?

Someone who makes panths (pants).

Why was the little horse unhappy?

Because every time it wanted something, its mother would say, "Neigh."

What did the pen say to the paper?
"I dot an 'i' on you."

What did the paper say to the pencil?
"Write on!"

When are club dues paid?
On Duesday (Tuesday).

What Roman numeral can climb a wall?
IV (ivy).

What do you get if you use a natural suntan lotion?
A Puritan (a purer tan).

Where do pencils come from?
From Pennsylvania.

What kind of tie does a pig wear?
A pigsty (pig's tie).

Why is an inexpensive dog a bad watchdog?
Because a bargain (barkin') dog does not bite.

What does a duck wear when he gets married?
A duxedo (tuxedo).

What fruit would a gorilla like to sleep on?
An ape-ri-cot (apricot).

Why do people feel stronger on Saturdays and Sundays?
Because all the other days are week (weak) days.

How can you spell chilly with two letters?
IC (icy).

What are two fibs?
A paralyze (pair of lies).

What did the beaver say to the tree?
"It's been nice gnawing (knowing) you."

Spell electricity with three letters.
NRG (energy).

What did the buffalo say to his son when he went away on a long trip?
"Bison!" ("Bye, son!")

What kind of ant can count?
An accountant.

What is an ant dictator?
A tyrant.

What is a bee?
An insect that stings (sings) for its supper.

What do you call a bee born in May?
A maybe.

What color was the "Keep off the Grass" sign?
G'way (gray).

When is a well-dressed lion like a weed?
When he's a dandelion (dandy lion).

What letter stands for a drink?
The letter T.

How many ghosts are there
in the nation?
*There must be a lot
ghost-to-ghost (coast-to-
coast).*

What geometric figure is
like a runaway parrot?
A polygon (Polly gone).

Do moths cry?
*Sure. Haven't you ever
seen a mothball (bawl)?*

Why is a pig's tail like 5 A.M.?
They are both twirly (too early).

What animal is a cannibal?
An anteater (aunt eater).

Why does a lion kneel before it springs?
Because it is preying (praying).

Where did the rancher take the sheep?
To the bah-bah (barber) shop.

What animal would you like to be on a cold day?
A little otter (hotter).

What did the werewolf write on his Christmas cards?
"Best vicious (wishes) of the season."

Can you spell a pretty girl with two letters?
QT (cutey).

What did one raindrop say to the other raindrop?
"My plop is bigger than your plop."

What did the bookworm say to the librarian?
"Can I burrow (borrow) this book?"

What kind of kitten works for the Red Cross?
A first-aid kit.

What newspaper do cows read?
The Daily Moos.

 # 4 Sick!

When is the vet busiest?
When it rains cats and dogs.

When don't you feel so hot?
When you catch a cold.

What means of transportation gives people colds?
A choo-choo train.

What is the difference between a bus driver and a cold?
One knows the stops, the other stops the nose.

Why does a dentist seem moody?
Because he always looks down in the mouth.

What would you call a small wound?
A short cut.

Which eye gets hit the most?
A bullseye.

When a girl slips on the ice, why can't her brother help her up?
He can't be a brother and assist her (a sister) too.

What kind of television program tells you who just broke an arm or leg?

A newscast.

How can you tell if a mummy has a cold?

He starts coffin.

What is the difference between a hill and a pill?

A hill is hard to get up, a pill is hard to get down.

What is the famous last word in surgery?

"Ouch!"

Why did the germ cross the microscope?

To get to the other side.

What sickness do cowboys get from riding wild horses?

Bronchitis (bronc-itis).

Why did the fireplace call the doctor?

Because the chimney had the flu (flue).

Why do your eyes look different when you come from an eye doctor?

Because they've been checked.

Why is a pony like a person with a sore throat?

Because they are both a little hoarse (horse).

Why did the doctor give up his practice?

Because he lost his patience (patients).

How do you know that peanuts are fattening?
Have you ever seen a skinny elephant?

How do you make a thin person fat?
Throw him up in the air and he comes down "Plump."

What do you get if an ax hits your head?
A splitting headache.

When they take out an appendix, it's an appendectomy; when they remove your tonsils, it's a tonsillectomy. What is it when they remove a growth from your head?
A haircut.

Why was the chicken sick?
It had people pox.

How did the clock feel when no one wound it up?
Run down.

How can you keep from getting a sharp pain in your eye when you drink chocolate milk?
Take the spoon out of the glass.

What is a sick crocodile?
An illigator.

Why did the secretary cut her fingers off?
She wanted to write shorthand.

If you don't feel well, what do you probably have?
A pair of gloves on your hands.

Why are doctors stingy?
First they say they will treat you, and then they make you pay for it.

What is the difference between a boxer and a man with a cold?
A boxer knows his blows, a man with a cold blows his nose.

What do cowboys call a doctor's hypodermic needle?
A sick (six) shooter.

If you fell off a ladder, what would you fall against?
Against your will.

What do you get if you put your head in a washing machine?
Cleaner and brighter thoughts.

When is the best time to buy a thermometer?
In the winter, because then it is lower.

What is the best thing to take when you're run over?
The number of the car that hit you.

What is better than presence of mind in an automobile accident?
Absence of body.

What did the doctor say to the tonsil?
"You look so cute, I think I'll take you out."

What has fifty legs but can't walk?
Half a centipede.

What is worse than a centipede with sore feet?
A giraffe with a sore throat.

What is worse than a giraffe with a sore throat?
A turtle with claustrophobia.

What is worse than a turtle with claustrophobia?
An elephant with hay fever.

Why shouldn't you make jokes about a fat person?
Because it's not nice to poke fun at someone else's expanse (expense).

What do seven days of dieting do?
They make one weak (week).

What is the best way to lose weight?
Learn to play the piano, and you can pound away all you want.

You never catch cold going up in an elevator. True or false?
True. You come down with a cold, never up.

If an apple a day keeps the doctor away, what will an onion do?
Keep everyone away.

What kind of animal needs oiling?
A mouse. It squeaks.

What happens when a pony gets sunburned?
You get a little horseradish (reddish).

Why did the farmer take the cow to the vet?
Because she was so mooo-dy.

What do you have if your head is hot, your feet are cold, and you see spots in front of your eyes?
You probably have a polka-dotted sock over your head.

Where do squirrels go when they have nervous break-downs?

To the nut house.

What did Frankenstein say when a bolt of lightning hit him?

"Thanks, I needed that!"

When do you have acute pain?

When you own a very pretty window.

How did the bread feel when it was put in the toaster?

It was burned up.

What did the doctor find when he examined the X-ray of the dummy's head?

Nothing.

If you dropped a tomato on your toe, would it hurt much?

Yes, if it were in a can.

When was medicine first mentioned in the Bible?
When Moses received the two tablets.

What did the tooth say to the dentist?
"Fill 'er up!"

Why can't a very thin person stand up straight?
Because he is lean.

What goes, "Ho, ho, ho, plop!"?
Santa Claus laughing his head off.

What happened when the dog swallowed the watch?
He got a lot of ticks.

How did the kid get a flat nose?

His teacher told him to keep it to the grindstone.

Did you hear the story about the germ?

Never mind. I don't want it spread all over.

What is a drill sergeant?

An army dentist.

Where do sick steamships go?

To the dock (doc).

Why is a fishing hook like the measles?

Because it's catching.

Why is Congress like a cold?

Because sometimes the ayes (eyes) have it and sometimes the no's (nose).

Why did the invisible mother take her invisible child to the doctor?

To find out why he wasn't all there.

What would happen if you swallowed uranium?

You would get atomic ache (a stomach ache).

What is the healthiest kind of water?

Well water.

What is the perfect cure for dandruff?

Baldness.

What did the dentist say to the golfer?
"You have a hole in one."

Why did the kid put his hand in the fuse box when the weather got hot?
He heard that fuses blew.

How did the skeleton know it was raining?
He could feel it in his bones.

What did the nervous kid say when the doctor asked if he had been getting enough iron?
"Yes, I chew my nails every day."

What does every drowning person say no matter what language he speaks?
"Glub, glub!"

Why is an eye doctor like a teacher?
They both test the pupils.

Why is a horse with a sore throat twice as sick as any other animal?
Because he is then a hoarse horse.

What happened when the icicle landed on the man's head?
It knocked him cold.

What do you get if you put your hand in a pot?
A potted palm.

Where do animals go when they lose their tails?
To a retail store.

What did the doctor say to the patient when he finished the operation?
"That's enough out of you."

What did the woman say when the doctor asked if she smoked cigarettes?
"Of cough!"

How can you tell if you are cross-eyed?
When you see eye-to-eye with yourself.

How do you know that army sergeants have a lot of headaches?
Because they always yell, "Tension!"

What is the best way to cure acid indigestion?
Stop drinking acid.

Why do you feel soft in the head when you wash your hair?

Because you get a soggy noodle.

What did the farmer use to cure his sick hog?

Oinkment (ointment).

Why did the man hit his hand with a hammer?

He wanted to see something swell.

What do you call a person who doesn't have all his fingers on one hand?

Normal. Fingers are supposed to be on two hands.

Why did the mother ghost take her ghost child to the doctor?

She was worried because he was in such good spirits.

What is the difference between a person asleep and a person awake?

With some people it's hard to tell the difference.

What nuts give you a cold?

Cachoo (cashew) nuts.

What happened when the horse swallowed a dollar bill?

He bucked.

What game do you play if you don't take care of your teeth?

Tooth (truth) or Consequences.

Why did the timid soul tiptoe past the medicine cabinet?

He didn't want to wake up the sleeping pills.

How was the blind carpenter able to see?

He picked up his hammer and saw.

How can you tell if a bucket is not well?

When it is a little pale (pail).

5 Goodies & Baddies

What do you call a sheep that is covered with chocolate?
A Hershey baaa (bar).

What kind of gun does a bee shoot?
A bee-bee gun.

Who supervises children when they play games?
The game warden.

What do witches eat?
Halloweenies (hollow wienies).

What criminal doesn't take baths?
A dirty crook.

What insect is religious?
A praying mantis.

What dog is religious?
A prairie dog.

Why did the man hit the clock?
Because the clock struck first.

Why do surgeons wear masks during operations?
Because if they make a mistake, no one will know who did it.

What did the big toe say to the little toe?
"There's a big heel following us."

How do you make an eggroll (egg roll)?
Push it.

Did you hear the story about the burp?
Never mind. It's not worth repeating.

What kind of music does a ghost like?
Haunting melodies.

Why is it dangerous to do math in the jungle?
If you add 4 and 4, you get 8.

If you want to learn how to fight, what book should you read?
A scrapbook.

What is yellow and wears a mask?
The Lone Lemon.

What is a pie in the sky?
A flying pizza.

What did the mother elephant say to the baby elephant when it misbehaved?
"Tusk, tusk!"

Why did the farmer plant sugar cubes?
Because he wanted to raise cane.

Why did the little girl eat bullets?
She wanted her hair to grow in bangs.

What kind of long-distance calls do ministers make when they speak to each other?
Parson-to-parson (person-to-person).

How are a bad boy and a canoe alike?
They both get paddled.

If you cross a bee and chopped meat, what do you get?
A humburger.

Why did the orchestra have bad manners?
Because it didn't know how to conduct itself.

Why is mayonnaise never ready?
Because it is always dressing.

What did the banana do when the monkey chased it?
The banana split.

What is a crazy pickle?
A daffydill.

What do ghosts eat for lunch?
Boo-loney (bologna) sandwiches.

Why did the jelly roll?
Because it saw the apple turnover.

What kind of cake should you serve to chicken?
Layer cake.

What kind of eggs does a wicked chicken lay?
Deviled eggs.

What did the chicken say when it was put in the pot?
"Boy, am I in hot water!"

What hired killer never goes to jail?
The exterminator.

How do you make Mexican chili?
Take him to the North Pole.

Why is a robber strong?
Because he holds people up.

Why was the invisible mother upset with her invisible child?
Because he was always appearing.

What is a prizefighter's favorite drink?
Punch.

Which hand should you use to stir tea?
Neither. It is better to use a spoon.

What is small, purple and dangerous?
A grape with a machine gun.

How can you tell if there is an elephant sleeping in your bed?

Look for peanut shells.

How can you keep a barking dog quiet?
With hush puppies.

What do you get when two strawberries meet?
A strawberry shake.

Why are Egyptian children good children?
Because they respect their mummies.

What is a hippie mummy?
A deady-o.

What did the father mummy say to the kid mummy when he asked for candy?
"You just had some a century ago!"

How do you know if a soda is any good?
A little swallow tells you.

What cruel person would sit on a baby?
A baby sitter.

What gun does a police dog use?
A dogmatic.

What is a policeman's favorite snack?
Copcakes (cupcakes).

Who is Count Dracula's favorite person on a base-ball team?
The bat boy.

Where do tough chickens come from?
From hard-boiled eggs.

How is a bell obedient?
It sounds off only when it is told (tolled).

What happens when a ghost is set on fire?
You get roast ghost.

How can you tell if there is an elephant in the refrigerator?
The door won't shut.

How can you tell if an elephant has been in the refrigerator?
By the footprints in the butter.

How does a hot dog speak?
Frankly.

What is a ghost's favorite drink in hot weather?
Ice-ghoul (cool) lemonade.

How did the girl zombie know the boy zombie liked her?
He said, "You really kill me."

What did the girl spirit say to the boy spirit?
"You don't stand a ghost of a chance with me."

What kind of food do brave soldiers eat?
Hero sandwiches.

When does a police dog not look like a police dog?
When it is an undercover agent.

What is stolen candy?
Hot chocolate.

What is round and has a bad temper?
A vicious circle.

How can you get rich by eating?
Eat fortune cookies.

Why do werewolves do well at school?
Because they give snappy answers.

What do well-behaved young lambs say to their mothers?
"Thank ewe!"

What did the mother ghost say to the child ghost?
"Don't spook until you're spooken to."

What is the last thing you eat before you die?
You bite the dust.

What kind of thief steals meat?
A hamburglar.

What did the burglar give his wife for her birthday?
A stole.

What did the apple say to the apple pie?
"You've got some crust."

What is a jittery sorceress?
A twitch.

How can you calm down an angry dragon breathing smoke and fire?

Throw water at him and he will let off steam.

What dog has bad manners?

A pointer—pointing is not polite.

When do crooks wear suspenders?

When they are holdup men.

What kind of bird do crooks hate?

A stool pigeon.

What do you get if you cross an elephant with a Boy Scout?

An elephant that helps old ladies cross the street.

What would happen if an elephant sat in front of you at the movies?

You would miss most of the show.

Why did the elephant wear sunglasses?

With all the silly elephant riddles around, he didn't want to be recognized.

What is Count Dracula's favorite snack?

A fangfurter (frankfurter).

What is Dracula's favorite ice cream dish?

A bloody sundae.

What kind of cookie must be handled carefully?
Ginger snaps.

What kind of person loves cocoa?
A coconut.

Why do dentists like potatoes?
Because they are so filling.

When is it polite to serve milk in a saucer?
When you feed the cat.

If you cross a cat and a pickle, what do you have?
A picklepuss.

What is the one room a zombie's house doesn't need?
A living room.

Why are vampires unpopular?
Because they are a pain in the neck.

What kind of monster is never around when you need him?
A werewolf because you always say, "Werewolf (where wolf)?"

What did the mother ghost tell the kid ghost when he went out to play?
"Don't get your sheets dirty!"

What happens to naughty pigs?
They become deviled ham.

6 Fooling Mother Nature

Why was the mother flea so sad?
  Because her children were going to the dogs.

What do you call nervous insects?
  Jitterbugs.

What do people do in China when it rains?
  Let it rain.

What is a dimple?
  A pimple going the other way.

What is black and yellow and goes zzub, zzub?
  A bee going backwards.

What is the snappiest snake?
  A garter snake.

Why are cards like wolves?
  Because they belong to a pack.

What do you get if you cross a worm and a fur coat?
  A caterpillar.

What do you get if you cross a kangaroo and a raccoon?

A fur coat with pockets.

What do you get if you cross a skunk and a bee?
An animal that stinks as it stings.

Why do the hippies study the stars?
Because they are so far out.

If an electric train travels 90 miles an hour in a westerly direction and the wind is blowing from the north, in which direction is the smoke blowing?
There is no smoke from an electric train!

What insect is like the top of a house?
A tick (attic).

What is a foreign ant?
Important.

Why are spiders like tops?
Because they are always spinning.

When does a female deer need money?
When she doesn't have a buck.

What is the difference between a train and a teacher?
A train goes "Choo-choo," but a teacher tells you to take the gum out of your mouth.

Why didn't the man believe what the sardine said?
It sounded too fishy.

Why are mosquitoes annoying?
Because they get under your skin.

Why do flies walk on the ceiling?
If they walked on the floor, someone might step on them.

What did the dirt say to the rain?
"If this keeps up, my name will be mud."

What kind of leopard has red spots?
A leopard with measles.

Where do black birds drink?
At a crowbar.

What is an easy way to make your money bigger?
Put it under a magnifying glass.

Why is the letter "A" like a flower?
Because a bee (B) comes after it.

How can you shorten a bed?
Don't sleep long in it.

If we breathe oxygen in the daytime, what do we breathe at night?
Nitrogen.

Why did the nature lover plant bird seed?
He wanted to grow canaries.

Why did the farmer plant old car parts in his garden?
He wanted to raise a bumper crop.

If a farmer raises wheat in dry weather, what does he raise in wet weather?
An umbrella.

What is a hot and noisy duck?
A firequacker.

What kind of horse comes from Pennsylvania?
A filly (Philly).

What do you always leave behind because they are dirty?

Your footprints.

Why is a rabbit's nose always shiny?

Because his powder puff is on the wrong end.

What is the difference between an oak tree and a tight shoe?

One makes acorns, the other makes corns ache.

What is the best way to raise strawberries?

With a spoon.

Why is a garden like a story?

They both have plots.

Why should you never tell secrets in a garden?

Because the corn has ears, the potatoes have eyes, and the beans talk (beanstalk).

Why do gardeners hate weeds?
Give weeds an inch and they'll take a yard.

What kind of person is fed up with people?
A cannibal.

If there were ten cats in a boat and one jumped out,
how many would be left?
None, because they were all copycats.

If a rooster laid a brown egg and a white egg, what
kind of chicks would hatch?
None. Roosters don't lay eggs.

How can you eat an egg without breaking its shell?
Ask someone else to break it.

What did one shrub say to the other shrub?
"Am I bushed!"

What did the tree say to the ax?
"I'm stumped."

What did the cotton plant say to the farmer?
"Stop picking on me!"

When can't astronauts land on the moon?
When it is full.

What is a ticklish subject?
The study of feathers.

What is the dirtiest word in the world?
Pollution.

How can a leopard change his spots?
Move to another place.

How can you tell where a bear lives?
Look for his Denmark (den mark).

Why does a baby duck walk softly?
Because it is a baby and it can't walk, hardly.

When you take away two letters from this five-letter
word, you get one. What word is it?
Stone.

What helps keep your teeth together?
Toothpaste.

Why are country people smarter than city people?
Because the population is denser in big cities.

What do Indians raise that you can get lost in?
Maize (maze).

What kind of fish performs operations?
A sturgeon (surgeon).

In what way are the letter "A" and noon the same?
Both are in the middle of day.

Why is it so wet in Great Britain?
Because of all the kings and queens that reigned (rained) there.

What bunch of animals can always be heard?
Cattle, because they go around in herds.

What do you call cattle that sit on the grass?
Ground beef.

Why shouldn't you cry if your cow falls off a mountain?
There's no use in crying over spilt milk.

"Did you hear the story about the peacock?"
"It's a beautiful tail (tale)."

What is the brightest fish?
Sunfish.

What brings the monster's babies?
Frankenstork.

What advice can you give a fish so he can avoid being caught?
Don't fall for any old line.

What are arithmetic bugs?
Mosquitoes. They add to misery, subtract from pleasure, divide your attention, and multiply quickly.

What animal talks a lot?
A yak.

What animal talks the most?
A yackety-yak.

How can you keep a rooster from crowing on Monday morning?

Eat him for dinner on Sunday.

What was the highest mountain before Mt. Everest was discovered?

Mt. Everest.

What goes snap, crackle, pop?

A firefly with a short circuit.

What did the father firefly say to his son?

"For a little fellow you're very bright."

What did one firefly say to the other firefly when his light went out?

"Give me a push. My battery is dead."

What has a head, a tail, four legs, and sees equally from both ends?

A blind mule.

How do birds stop themselves in the air?

With air brakes.

Why is it dangerous to walk around the country in the spring?

Because then the grass is full of blades, the flowers have pistils (pistols), and the trees are shooting.

Why do cows wear bells?

Because their horns don't work.

How did the big mountain know that the little mountain was fibbing?

Because it was only a bluff.

What is nothing but holes tied to holes, yet is as strong as iron?

A chain.

What happens to grapes that worry too much?

They get wrinkled and turn into raisins.

What did the bald man say when he got a comb?

"I'll never part with it."

What did Ben Franklin say when he discovered that lightning was electricity?

Nothing. He was too shocked.

What is the difference between lightning and electricity?

We pay for electricity.

What children live in the ocean?

Life buoys (boys).

What insect curses in a low voice?
A locust.

What insects talk too much?
Moths. They are always chewing the rag.

How do you know that bees are happy?
Because they hum while they work.

Why do bees hum?
Because they don't know the words.

What did the mother worm say to the little worm who was late?
"Where in earth have you been?"

What did one termite say to the other termite when he saw a house burning?
"Barbecue tonight!"

What did the grasshopper say to the cockroach?
"Bug, you man me!"

Why don't bananas snore?
They don't want to wake up the rest of the bunch.

Who settled in the West before anyone else?
The sun.

How can you tune into the sun?
Use a sundial.

Which is more important, the sun or the moon?
The moon. It shines when it is dark, but the sun shines when it is light anyway.

What kind of pigeon sits down a lot?
A stool pigeon.

How can you tell that a cat likes the rain?
Because when it rains it purrs (pours).

Why is a cat like a penny?
Because it has a head on one side and a tail on the other.

What is a distant relative?
Someone who is not living with you.

Why did the lady mouse want to move?
She was tired of living in a hole in the wall.

Why do squirrels spend so much time in trees?
To get away from all the nuts on the ground.

How do rabbits keep their fur neat?
They use a harebrush (hairbrush).

Who was older, David or Goliath?
David must have been because he rocked Goliath to sleep.

How can you fix a short circuit?
Lengthen it.

What did one toad say to the other toad?
"One more game of leapfrog and I'll croak."

What did the coughing frog say to the other frog?
"I must have a person in my throat."

What did the porcupine say to the cactus?
"Are you my mother?"

Why don't flies fly through screen doors?
Because they don't want to strain themselves.

What animals didn't come on the ark in pairs?
Worms. They came in apples.

If you throw a pumpkin in the air, what comes down?
Squash.

During what season do ants eat most?
Summer. That is when they go to a lot of picnics.

What sea creature has to have a good reason for doing anything?
A porpoise (purpose).

What is the correct thing to do before the King of Trees?
Bough (bow).

7 World Records

What is the biggest ant?
An elephant.

What is the biggest building?
The library. It has the most stories.

Which American had the biggest family?
George Washington, because he was the father of his country.

Who is the biggest liar in the world?
A rodeo man, because he is always trying to throw the bull.

When the biggest elephant in the world fell into a 30-foot well, how did they get it out?
Wet.

What is as big as an elephant but doesn't weigh anything?
An elephant's shadow.

What is the best way to catch an elephant?
Act like a nut and he'll follow you anywhere.

What has a big mouth but doesn't say a word?
A river.

Who was the biggest thief in history?
Atlas, because he held up the whole world.

What is the biggest fly swatter?
A baseball bat.

What is the best way to hold a bat?
By the wings.

How can you spell too much with two letters?
XS (excess).

When does a mouse weigh as much as an elephant?
When the scale is broken.

Who wears the smallest hat?
A narrow-minded person.

What word grows smaller when you add two letters to it?
Add "er" to short and it becomes shorter.

What is a midget skunk called?
A shrunk skunk.

What is smaller than an ant's mouth?
An ant's dinner.

What is the distance between a stupid person's ears?
Next to nothing.

What is a very small frankfurter?
An itsy bitsy, teeny wienie.

What is a small laugh in Indian language?
A Minnehaha.

What dog is 100 years old?
A sentry (century) dog.

What is the longest word in the English language?
"Smiles," because there is a "mile" between the first and last letters.

What is the longest shortest word?
Abbreviation.

Why is the longest human nose on record only 11 inches long?
Because if it were 12 inches long it would be a foot.

What is the longest view in the world?
Down a road with telephone poles, because then you can see from pole to pole.

What kind of clothing wears the longest?
Underwear, because it is never worn out.

When is a miniskirt long?
When a midget wears it.

What is the shortest month?
May. It has only three letters.

What is the craziest tree?
A knotty (nutty) pine.

What kind of pine has
the sharpest needles?
Porcupine.

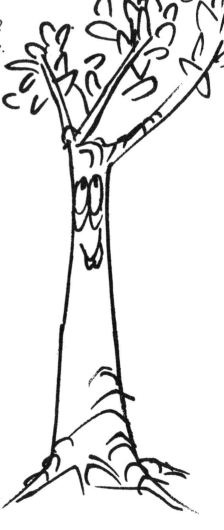

What flower is happiest?
Gladiola.

What is the hottest day
of the week?
Friday (Fry day).

What is the hottest part
of a man's face?
His sideburns.

What side of a fire is
the hottest?
The fireside.

When was beef at its highest?
When the cow jumped over the moon.

What fish has the lowest voice?
A bass.

What person adds best in hot weather?
A summer.

What is the laziest mountain in the world?
Mt. Everest.

What are the laziest animals on the farm?
Chickens. They are always laying (lying) around.

What is the most tired vegetable?
A beet (beat).

What is the poorest plant?
A vine, because it can't support itself.

What birds are noisiest?
Whooping cranes.

What person has the loudest voice?
The ice cream (I scream) man.

What is the smartest animal?
A skunk, because it makes a lot of scents (sense).

Which is faster, hot or cold?
Hot, because you can catch cold.

What animal grows the fastest?

A kangaroo. It grows by leaps and bounds.

What was the greatest invention in the world?

The wheel because it got everything rolling.

What kind of house weighs the least?

A lighthouse.

Who was the strongest man in the Bible?

Jonah. Even the whale couldn't keep him down.

Why did the farmer think he was the strongest man in the world?

Because he raised a 600-pound pig.

Who is the strongest thief?

A shoplifter.

What is the strongest animal?

The snail because it carries its house on its back.

Who has the strongest fingers in the world?

A miser because he is always pinching pennies.

What is the most important subject a witch learns in witch school?

Spelling.

Why is the letter N the most powerful letter?

Because it is in the middle of TNT.

Who is the most musical grandfather you could have?
One who fiddles with his beard.

Where can you find the largest diamond in the world?
On a baseball field.

What is the biggest baseball team?
The Giants.

In what part of a ballpark do you find the whitest clothes?

In the bleachers.

What are the best kind of stockings for baseball players to wear?

Stockings with runs in them.

Where is the headquarters for the Umpire's Association?

The Umpire (Empire) State Building.

What is the quietest sport?

Bowling, because you can hear a pin drop.

What is the loudest sport?

Tennis, because everyone raises a racquet (racket).

What is the hardest thing about learning to roller skate?

The ground.

What is the easiest way to make a banana split?

Cut it in half.

What disease makes you better in sports?
Athlete's foot.

When is a boat cheapest?
When it is a sail (sale) boat.

Why is a kid who plays all day in a marathon like a phonograph record?
Because he is long-playing.

What coat has the most sleeves?
A coat of arms.

What is the easiest way to grow tall?
Sleep long.

What is more invisible than an invisible man?
The shadow of an invisible man.

What is the best way to find a pin in a rug?
Walk around in your bare feet.

What is the best way to catch a squirrel?
Climb up a tree and act like a nut.

What is the best thing to put into a pie?
Your teeth.

What is the best key to have?
Lucky.

Who is the fattest female phantom?
The ghostess with the mostest.

How did the 800-pound man feel when he lost 250 pounds?

Delighted.

Why is being fat not very funny?

Because you can't laugh it off.

An elephant always remembers, but what kind of animal always forgets?

An owl because it keeps saying, "Who? Who?"

What dog does not bark no matter what you do to him?

A hot dog.

Why is a hot dog the best dog?

Because it doesn't bite the hand that feeds it but feeds the one that bites it.

Why is the Dracula family so close?

Because blood is thicker than water.

What fruit has been known since man invented the calendar?

Dates.

What cake is as hard as a rock?

Marble cake.

What food do monster children hate most?

Cremated (creamed) spinach.

8 Mad Mad Mad

How does a witch tell time?
With a witch watch.

Who drives away all of his customers?
A taxicab driver.

What driver doesn't have a license?
A screw driver.

What do you call a high-priced barber shop?
A clip joint.

If you cross a telephone and a pair of scissors, what
do you get?
Snippy answers.

If you cross a telephone and a lobster what will you
get?
Snappy talk.

Who is bigger, Mrs. Bigger or her baby?
Her baby is a little Bigger.

What is purple and 5,000 miles long?
The Grape Wall of China.

What is green, has two legs and a trunk?
A seasick tourist.

What do you call an Indian woman who complains a lot?
A squaw-ker.

What kind of ears do trains have?
Engineers (engine ears).

Why does a dog have fur?
If it didn't, it would be a little bare (bear).

What game is played in the bathroom?
Ring around the tub.

Why shouldn't you tell secrets when a clock is around?
Because time will tell.

What is a drill team?
A group of dentists who work together.

Where can you always find health, wealth and happiness?
In the dictionary.

What is an astronaut's favorite meal?
Launch.

What can you serve but never eat?
A tennis ball.

What kind of tables do people eat?
Vegetables.

Why do we dress baby girls in pink and baby boys in blue?
Because they can't dress themselves.

What is the difference between an umbrella and a person who never stops talking?
The umbrella can be shut up.

Why do people buy things with their credit cards?
They get a charge out of it.

What is the most important use for cowhide?
It helps keep the cow together.

Who was the first to have a mobile home?
A turtle.

What is a wisecrack?
An educated hole in the wall.

What kind of fence goes on strike?
A picket fence.

A man who worked in the butcher shop was 6 feet tall, had red hair and wore size 11 shoes. What did he weigh?
Meat.

What is lemonade?
When you help an old lemon cross the street.

What socks do you find in your back yard?
Garden hose.

What has a head, can't think, but drives?
A hammer.

Where do young country dogs sleep?
In pup tents.

What kind of test does a vampire take in school?
A blood test.

What is the best way to prevent milk from turning sour?
Leave it in the cow.

How does a coffee pot feel when it is hot?
Perky.

What is blue, green, yellow, purple, brown, black, and grey?
A box of crayons.

How can you make any watch a stopwatch?
Don't wind it.

What do you do with dogs when you go shopping?
Leave them in the barking (parking) lot.

What is a dog catcher?
A Spot remover.

What did the two vampires do from midnight to 12:10?
They took a coffin (coffee) break.

How can you make money fast?
Glue it to the floor.

How can you make a soup rich?
Add 14 carrots (carats) to it.

Why did the hippie put his money in the refrigerator?
He liked cold cash.

What happened when the man asked the salesman for a good belt?
"O.K., you asked for it," the salesman said as he gave him a good belt.

How does a pair of pants feel when it is ironed?
Depressed.

Why was the shoe unhappy?
Because his father was a loafer and his mother a sneaker.

What did one skunk say to the other?
"So do you!"

What did one pig say to the other pig?
"Let's be pen pals."

What did the fly say when he landed on the book?
"I think I read this story before."

Why can't a bicycle stand up by itself?
Because it is two-tired (too tired).

What is 10+5 minus 15? What is 3+6 minus 9? What is 17+3 minus 20?
All that work for nothing!

What do people in England call little black cats?
Kittens.

If Washington's wife went to Washington while Washington's washwoman washed Washington's woolies, how many W's are there in all?

None. There are no W's in "all."

How do you make a Venetian blind?

Stick a finger in his eye.

Where did the three little kittens find their mittens?

In the Yellow Pages.

What is the difference between twice twenty-two and twice two and twenty?

One is 44, the other is 24.

Why do they say George Washington was an orphan?
He was the foundling father of his country.

Why do they say George Washington couldn't swim?
He was the foundering father of his country.

Why was George Washington like a fish?
He was the flounder of his country.

When does a bed grow longer?
At night, because two feet are added to it.

What is the best way to cure someone who walks in his sleep?
Put tacks on the floor.

Why do lions eat raw meat?
Because they don't know how to cook.

What kind of car do werewolves buy?
A Wolfswagen.

What would you call a grandfather clock?
An old timer.

How many letters are there in the alphabet?
Eleven. T-H-E A-L-P-H-A-B-E-T.

Did Adam and Eve ever have a date?
No, they had an apple.

What kind of nut has no shell?
A doughnut.

What is a stupid flower?
A blooming idiot.

What can you do with old bowling balls?
Give them to elephants to shoot marbles.

Why couldn't Humpty Dumpty be put together again?
Because he wasn't everything he was cracked up to be.

In a certain city there is a corner with four stores. One is a bakery, one a candy store, one a drugstore, and one a bookstore. Outside the drugstore is a policeman. Why is the policeman called Oscar?
Because that is his name.

Dogs have fleas. What do sheep have?
Fleece.

What room can you bounce around in?
A ballroom.

What is a bulldozer?
Someone who sleeps while a politican is making a speech.

Where do ghosts go for fresh air?
To the sea ghost (coast).

How can you tell when there is an elephant in your sandwich?
When it is too heavy to lift.

How do you fit five elephants into a Volkswagen?
Two in the front, two in the back, and one in the glove compartment.

What fish did the knights eat?
Swordfish.

What fish do pelicans eat?
Anything that fits the bill.

What would happen if you swallowed a frog?
You might croak.

Where do trees keep their money?
In branch banks.

Where do hogs keep their money?
In piggy banks.

Where do Eskimos keep their money?
In snowbanks.

Where do fish keep their money?
In river banks.

Where do vampires keep their money?
In blood banks.

What is the best way to get rid of flies?
Sign up some good outfielders.

"Where did Abraham Lincoln live?"
"I have his Gettysburg Address right here!"

If cheese comes on top of a hamburger, what comes after cheese?
A mouse.

Where do mummies swim?
In the Dead Sea.

What is the best way to eat spaghetti?
First, open your mouth.

The alphabet goes from A to Z. What goes from Z to A?

Zebra.

What has a head but no brain?

A cabbage.

What is a grasshopper?

An insect on a pogo stick.

What did one mountain say to the other mountain after an earthquake?

"It's not my fault."

What did the boy centipede say to the girl centipede?

"You sure have a nice pair of legs, pair of legs, pair of legs . . ."

What did the little light bulb say to its mother?
"I wuv you watts and watts."

What is the best way to make pants last?
Make the jacket first.

What makes more noise than a squealing pig?
Two squealing pigs.

What happened when Abel died?
He became unable.

Why do wallets make so much noise?
Because money talks.

What happens to a refrigerator when you pull its plug?
It loses its cool.

What is a tongue twister?
When your tang gets all tongueled up.

When should you charge a new battery?
When you can't pay cash.

How many skunks does it take to make a big stink?
A phew (few).

Why did the invisible man look in the mirror?
To see if he still wasn't there.

What does an invisible baby drink?
Evaporated milk.

What runs around all day and then lies under the bed with its tongue hanging out?
Your shoe.

What is a briefcase?
A short law suit.

When does an Irish potato change nationality?
When it is French fried.

To whom did Paul Revere give his handkerchief?
To the town crier.

What did King Kong say when he saw the Statue of Liberty?
"Are you my mother?"

What is a bacteria?
The rear entrance of a cafeteria.

When is a bicycle not a bicycle?
When it turns into a driveway.

What is red and goes up and down?
A tomato in an elevator.

What lottery did the broom win?
The sweepstakes.

What keys won't open doors?
Don-keys, mon-keys, tur-keys.

9 Strange—But True

Why does a chicken lay an egg?
If she dropped it, it would break.

How can you drop an egg 3 feet without breaking it?
Drop it 4 feet. For the first 3 feet the egg will not hit anything.

Why is a room full of married couples empty?
Because there is not a single person in it.

What is the difference between a greedy person and an electric toaster?
One takes the most and the other makes the toast.

What man is strong enough to hold up a car with one hand?
A policeman.

Why do you always start to walk with the right foot first?
Because when you move one foot, the other one is always left-behind.

When do you swallow your words?
When you eat alphabet soup.

How can you be sure you have counterfeit money?
If it's a three-dollar bill, you can be sure.

What goes out black and comes in white?
A black cow in a snowstorm.

Is it better to write on a full or on an empty stomach?
Neither. Paper is much better.

Where do fish wash themselves?
In the river basin.

What can you add to a bucket of water that will make it weigh less?
Holes.

Where do cars get the most flat tires?
Where there is a fork in the road.

What kind of bird is always around when there is something to eat or drink?
A swallow.

Why don't scarecrows have any fun?
Because they are stuffed shirts.

How can you go without sleep for seven days and not be tired?
Sleep at night.

Why are identical twins like a broken alarm clock?
Because they are dead ringers.

What lands as often on its tail as it does its head?
A penny.

Why is the number nine like a peacock?
Because it is nothing without its tail.

What "bus" crossed the ocean?
Columbus.

What kind of tickle doesn't make you laugh?
A tickle in your throat.

How do you make a cigarette lighter?
Take out the tobacco.

How do you make notes of stone?
Rearrange the letters.

What kind of pool can't you swim in?
A car pool.

Why are dogs like trees?
They both have barks.

What kind of umbrella does the Queen of England carry on a rainy day?

A wet one.

What goes through a door but never goes in or out?

A keyhole.

What can turn without moving?

Milk. It can turn sour.

What code message is the same from left to right, right to left, upside down and right side up?

S O S.

Why does the stork stand on one leg only?

If he lifted it, he would fall down.

How is a pig like a horse?
When a pig is hungry he eats like a horse, and when a horse is hungry he eats like a pig.

On which side does a chicken have the most feathers?
On the outside.

Why do you say that whales talk a lot?
Because they are always spouting off.

What invention allows you to see through walls?
A window.

What has two legs like an Indian, two eyes like an Indian, two hands like an Indian, looks just like an Indian—but is not an Indian?
The picture of an Indian.

What is the difference between a banana and a bell?
You can only peel (peal) the banana once.

What can a whole apple do that half an apple can't do?
It can look round.

How many acorns grow on the average pine tree?
None. Pine trees don't have acorns.

What is always behind the times?
The back of a clock.

When is a man not a man?
When he turns into an alley.

If April showers bring May flowers, what do the Mayflowers bring?

Pilgrims.

What baby is born with whiskers?

A kitten.

How should you treat a baby goat?

Like a kid.

What kind of coat has no sleeves, no buttons, no pockets and won't keep you warm?

A coat of paint.

What kind of fall makes you unconscious but doesn't hurt you?

Falling asleep.

What turns everything around but doesn't move?

A mirror.

What was the largest island in the world before Australia was discovered?

Australia.

How do we know Rome was built at night?

Because Rome wasn't built in day.

What lives in winter, dies in summer, and grows with its roots upwards?

An icicle.

Why do hummingbirds hum?
Because they can't read music.

What kind of pliers do you use in arithmetic?
Multipliers.

What has four fingers and thumb but is not a hand?
A glove.

What is the hardest thing about learning to skate?
The ice.

What has a hundred limbs but can't walk?
A tree.

What is the longest word in the world?
Rubber, because it stretches.

How much dirt is there in a hole exactly one foot deep and one foot across?

None. A hole is empty.

When will a net hold water?

When the water is frozen into ice.

What is locomotion?

A crazy dance.

If you had 5 potatoes and had to divide them equally between 3 people, what should you do?

Mash them first.

What do they do with a tree after they chop it down?

Chop it up.

When are eyes not eyes?
When the wind makes them water.

What is plowed but never planted?
Snow.

What did Columbus see on his right hand when he discovered America?
Five fingers.

How can you make a fire with only one stick?
Easy. Just make sure it's a matchstick.

Why is the letter B hot?
Because it makes oil boil.

If you take half from a half dollar, what do you have?
A dollar.

What is a dark horse?
A nightmare.

Why shouldn't you keep a library book on the ground overnight?
Because in the morning it will be overdue (dew).

What is on your arm and in the sea?
A muscle (mussel).

Every morning the farmer had eggs for breakfast. He owned no chickens and he never got eggs from anyone else's chickens. Where did he get the eggs?
From his ducks.

What animals follow everywhere you go?
Your calves.

What do elephants have that no other animals have?
Baby elephants.

What is shaped like a box, has no feet and runs up and down?
An elevator.

What is an Eskimo father?
A cold pop.

How is a burning candle like thirst?
A bit of water ends both of them.

What is never out of sight?
The letter S.

What happens if you talk when there is food in your mouth?
You will have said a mouthful.

What does grass say when it is cut?
"I don't mow (know)."

How are 2 plus 2 equal 5 and your left hand alike?
Neither is right.

What goes further the slower it goes?
Money.

What kind of bow can't be tied?

A rainbow.

Why doesn't it cost much to feed a horse?

Because a horse eats best when it doesn't have a bit in its mouth.

How many worms make a foot?

Twelve inchworms.

How many feet are in a yard?

It depends on how many people are standing in it.

What has a foot on each side and one in the middle?
A yardstick.

How do we know that mountain goats have feet?
Because they are sure-footed.

Why can't it rain for two nights in a row?
Because there is a day between.

What color is rain?
Water color.

What goes through water but doesn't get wet?
A ray of light.

What is a small cad?
A caddy.

What has a neck but no head?
A bottle.

Why is your nose in the middle of your face?
Because it is the scenter (center).

If an egg came floating down the Mississippi River, where did it come from?
From a chicken.

What can you put in a glass but never take out of it?
A crack.

Why do elephants have trunks?
Because they don't have pockets to put things in.

Why does the giraffe have a long neck?
Because his head is so far from his body.

Why is a pig in the house like a house afire?
Because the sooner you put it out, the better.

What goes from side to side, and up and down, but never moves?
A road.

What is pointed in one direction and headed in the other?
A pin.

What can you hold in your left hand but not in your right hand?
Your right elbow.

What is in the middle of March?
The letter R.

Which is better, an old ten dollar bill or a new one?
An old ten dollar bill is better than a new one.

What kind of car drives over water?
Any kind of car, if it goes over a bridge.

What is the difference between a truthful person and a liar?
One lies when he sleeps, the other lies all the time.

Two men dig a hole in five days. How many days would it take them to dig half a hole?
None. You can't dig half a hole.

What is dark but made by light?
A shadow.

How can you place a pencil on the floor so that no one can jump over it?
Put it next to the wall.

What increases its value by being turned upside down?
The number 6.

What do you lose every time you stand up?
Your lap.

When is a black dog not a black dog?
When it is a greyhound.

Where do children grow?
In a kindergarten.

Why is it so easy to weigh fish?
Because the fish have their own scales.

How many sides does a box have?
Two, the inside and the outside.

When can a man be 6 feet tall and short at the same time?
When he is short of money.

What is the center of gravity?
The letter V.

Is it better to say, "The yolk of an egg is white," or "The yolk of an egg are white?"

Neither. An egg yolk is yellow.

Why should a man's hair turn gray before his moustache?

Because it is older.

What kind of beans won't grow in a garden?

Jelly beans.

How many beans can you put in an empty bag?

One. After that the bag isn't empty.

When do you go as fast as a racing car?

When you are in it.

What is the difference between a racer and a locomotive engineer?

One is trained to run, the other runs a train.

From what number can you take half and leave nothing?

The number is 8. Take away the top half and o is left.

Which is more nourishing, a cow or a shooting star?

A shooting star, because it is meteor (meatier).

10 That's Entertainment

What is the easiest way to get on TV?
Sit on your set.

What happened to the kid who ran away with the circus?
The police made him bring it back.

Where did King Arthur go for entertainment?
To a nightclub (knight club).

What animals are poor dancers?
Four-legged ones, because they have two left feet.

Why couldn't anyone play cards on the ark?
Because Noah sat on the deck.

Why is a crossword puzzle like a quarrel?
Because one word leads to another.

What newspaper did the cavemen read?
The Prehistoric Times.

Where do snowflakes dance?
At the snowball.

Where do golfers dance?
At the golf ball.

Where do chickens dance?
At the fowl ball.

Where do butchers dance?
At the meatball.

What holiday does Dracula celebrate in November?
Fangsgiving (Thanksgiving).

What is a perfect name for a selfish girl?
Mimi (me, me).

What is a musical pickle?
A piccolo.

When do ghosts haunt skyscrapers?
When they are in high spirits.

What kind of inning does a monster baseball game have?
Frightening (fright inning).

Why are comedians like doctors?
Because they keep people in stitches.

Who has more fun when you tickle a mule?
He may enjoy it, but you'll get a bigger kick out of it.

Why did the owl make everyone laugh?
Because he was a howl.

Did you hear the story about the piece of butter?
Never mind. I don't want to spread it around.

What is the favorite ride of ghost children?
The roller ghoster (coaster).

Why can't an elephant ride a bicycle?
Because he doesn't have a thumb to ring the bell.

What amusement park ride breaks up romances?
A merry-go-round. When the ride is over, people stop going around with each other.

What kind of musician can't you trust?
Someone who plays the bull fiddle.

What kind of book does Frankenstein like to read?
A novel with a cemetery plot.

Where is the best place to have a bubble gum contest?
On a choo-choo train.

What is a car fender's favorite song?
"Fender (when the) Moon Shines Over the Mountain."

What is a horse's favorite song?
"Big Horse (because) I Love You."

What is a ghost's favorite song?
"A-Haunting We Will Go."

What is a boiling kettle's favorite song?
"Home on the Range."

What keeps out bugs and shows movies?
Screens.

What is green and sings?
Elvis Parsley.

Why are jazz musicians so sweet?
Because they play in jam sessions.

What is a fund for needy musicians?
A band aid.

What is in fashion but always out of date?
The letter F.

What broadcasting company has the best horror shows?
The Ghost-to-Ghost network.

Why is the circusman who was shot out of the cannon not working anymore?
Because he was discharged.

What kind of phone makes music?
A saxophone.

What did one firecracker say to the other firecracker?
"My pop is bigger than your pop."

What fish is famous?
A starfish.

Why are movie stars cool?
Because they have so many fans.

Why did the kid put a flashlight on his stomach?
He wanted to watch bellyvision (television).

Why was night baseball started?
Because bats like to sleep in the daytime.

What is as round as the moon, as black as coal, and has a hole in the middle?
A phonograph record.

Why was the phonograph record nervous?
You would be too if you lived on spins and needles.

Why is a phonograph needle like a chicken?
They both scratch.

What famous dance music did Charles Dickens write?
"Oliver Twist."

What dance do you do when summer is over?
Tango (tan go).

Why did the little kid dance on the jar of jam?
Because the top said, "Twist to open."

What is an opera?
In an opera people sing before they die.

What do you call someone who hates operas?
An operator (opera-hater).

Why do witches fly on broomsticks?
It beats walking.

What is the difference between a dancer and a duck?
One goes quick on her beautiful legs, the other goes quack on her beautiful legs.

What is the difference between a ballerina and a duck?
One dances Swan Lake, the other swims in it.

Why did the kid put his head on the piano?
Because he wanted to play by ear.

Why doesn't the piano work?
Because it only knows how to play.

Why are pianos so noble?
Many are upright and the rest are grand.

Why couldn't anyone find the famous composer?
Because he was Haydn (hidin').

Why did the girl call herself an experienced actress?
She broke her leg and was in a cast for six months.

What did the football say to the football player?
"I get a kick out of you."

Why did the football player marry the girl?
Because he thought she would be faithful to the end.

Why are good bowlers like labor unions?
Because they strike a lot.

What should you do if your dog swallows a book?
Take the words right out of his mouth.

What fish sings songs?
A tuna fish.

Who wrote, "Oh, say can you see?"
An eye doctor.

Why did the elephant paint himself all different colors?
So he could hide in the crayon box.

Who makes up jokes about knitting?
  A nitwit.

Why did the comedian tell jokes to the eggs?
  He wanted to crack them up.

Did you hear the story about the oatmeal?
  Never mind. It's a lot of mush.

Who was Mr. Ferris?
  He was a big wheel in the amusement park business.

Phil played the harmonica so well he now plays with what symphony orchestra?
  The Philharmonica.

If a band plays music in a thunderstorm, who is most likely to get hit by lightning?
  The conductor.

What kind of band doesn't make music?
  A rubber band.

What game do you play in water?
  Swimming pool.

What game do ghost children play?
  Haunt and seek.

What season is it when you are on a trampoline?
  Springtime.

What is a vampire's favorite song?
"Fangs (thanks) for the Memory."

What is the Eskimo's favorite song?
"Freeze (For he's) a Jolly Good Fellow."

Why did the boy get a dachshund?
Because his favorite song was, "Get Along Little Dogie."

Why did the tightrope walker always carry his bank book?
In order to check his balance.

What kind of girl does a mummy go out with?
Any girl he can dig up.

Where do mummies go when they visit Arizona?
The Petrified Forest.

What do birds say on Halloween?
"Twick or tweet."

Why did the mother put her baby on the phonograph?
It had an automatic changer.

What would you get if you crossed a stereo and a refrigerator?
Very cool music.

What musical instrument does a skeleton play?
The trombone.

Why was William Shakespeare able to write so well?
Because where there's a Will, there's a way.

What song was written by a lazy southern traveler?
"Carry Me Back to Old Virginny."

Why is Lassie like a comet?
They both are stars with tails.

What kind of flower does Lassie like?
A cauliflower (collie flower).

What kind of song is, "Soap, Soap, Soap, Soap, Soap?"
Five bars.

What has eight feet and can sing?
A barbershop quartet.

If you scratch a horse's hair on a cat gut, what do you get?
Violin music.*
*This is a fact. Violin bows use horse hair and violin strings are made of cat gut.

Why is a violin like an auto?
It is best when tuned up.

What large instrument do you carry in your ears?
Drums.

What kind of dance do buns do?
Abundance.

What is avoidance?
A dance for people who hate each other.

What dance do hippies hate?
A square dance.

How do they dance in Arabia?
Sheik-to-sheik (cheek).

What is a dance for two containers?
The can-can.

What dance did the Pilgrims do?
The Plymouth Rock.

Why did they have to put a fence around the cemetery?
Because so many people were dying to get in.

What song do monsters sing at Christmas time?
"Deck the halls with poison ivy,
Fal-la la, la-la . . ."

11 Riddles For Thinkers

Why is the world like a faulty jigsaw puzzle?
Because a peace (piece) is missing.

What can be caught and heard but never seen?
A remark.

What can be measured but has no length, width or thickness?
The temperature.

What gets harder to catch the faster you run?
Your breath.

A frog fell into a well 12 feet deep. He could jump 3 feet, but every time he jumped 3 feet, he fell back 2 feet. How many times did he have to jump to get out of the well?
The tenth jump took him out. (On the tenth jump he reached 13 feet and was out.)

What is the difference between a dog and a gossip?
One has a wagging tail, the other a wagging tongue.

Why does a dog wag his tail?
Because no one else will wag it for him.

What is the best way to clean up a dirty mind?
Think a litter bit less.

How long should a person's legs be?
Long enough to reach the ground.

What gets wetter the more it dries?
A towel.

What has 6 legs, but walks with only 4?
A horse with a rider.

What didn't Adam and Eve have that everyone else in the world has had?
Parents.

When is longhand quicker than shorthand?
On a clock.

Would you rather an elephant attacked you or a gorilla?
I'd rather he attacked the gorilla.

How does an elephant get down from a tree?
He sits on a leaf and waits for the fall.

When is your mind like a rumpled bed?
When it isn't made up yet.

On the way to a water hole a zebra met 6 giraffes.
Each giraffe had 3 monkeys hanging from its neck.
Each monkey had 2 birds on its tail. How many
animals were going to the water hole?
*Only the zebra. All the rest were coming back
from the hole.*

Who invented the first airplane that didn't fly?
The Wrong Brothers.

What did the sardine call the submarine?
   A can with people in it.

How many legs does a mule have if you call its tail
a leg?
   Only four. Calling a tail a leg doesn't make it one.

What can you break with only one word?
   Silence.

What has cities with no houses, rivers without water,
and forests without trees?
   A map.

What flies when it's on and floats when it's off?
   A feather.

What has a big mouth but can't talk?
A jar.

Spell extra wise in two letters.
YY (2 y's)

Almost everyone needs it, asks for it, gives it, but almost nobody takes it. What is it?
Advice.

What is brought to the table and cut, but never eaten?
A deck of cards.

What question can you never answer "yes" to?
"Are you asleep?"

Why is a poor friend better than a rich one?
Because a friend in need is a friend indeed.

Why is it interesting to study mummies?
Because you can get so wrapped up in them.

With what vegetable do you throw away the outside, cook the inside, eat the outside, and throw away the inside?
Corn on the cob.

What kind of tea helps you feel brave?
Safety.

Why do mother kangaroos hate rainy days?
Because then the children have to play inside.

How do we know the deer and the antelope are deaf?
Because they never heard a discouraging word.

How can you tell the difference between trees?
Listen to their barks.

What can't you see that is always before you?
The future.

What can you hold without your hands?
Your breath.

What can you give away and still keep?
A cold.

When is it correct to say, "I is?"
"I is the letter after H."

What word allows you to take away two letters and get one?
Alone.

What is boiled then cooled, sweetened then soured?
Iced tea with lemon.

If 5 cats catch 5 mice in 5 minutes, how long will it take one cat to catch a mouse?
Five minutes.

The more you crack it, the more people like you. What is it?
A smile.

What comes from a tree and fights cavities?
A toothpick.

What is the beginning of eternity,
The end of time and space;
The beginning of every end,
And the end of every race?
The letter E.

Why do dogs scratch themselves?
Because they are the only ones who know where it itches.

There is a secret Christmas message in the following letters. Can you find it? A, b, c, d, e, f, g, h, i, j, k, m, n, o, p, q, r, s, t, u, v, w, x, y, z.

No L (Noel).

Why didn't the skeleton kid want to go to school?

Because his heart wasn't in it.

What could you do if you were on a desert island without food or water?

Open your watch: drink from the spring, and eat the sand which is (sandwiches) there.

What dress does everyone have but no one wears?

Address.

What has no beginning or end and nothing in the middle?

A doughnut.

What is neither inside a house nor outside a house, but no house would be complete without it?

A window.

The more there is of it, the less you see it. What is it?

Darkness.

Name five days of the week without saying: Monday, Tuesday, Wednesday, Thursday, Friday.

The day before yesterday, yesterday, today, tomorrow, the day after tomorrow.

What overpowers you—without hurting you?

Sleep.

What is the first thing ghosts do when they get in a car?

They boo-ckle up.

A doctor and a boy were fishing. The boy was the doctor's son, but the doctor was not the boy's father. Who was the doctor?

His mother.

A man had 12 sheep. All but 9 died. How many sheep did he have left?

Nine.

How do you get down from an elephant?

You don't get down from an elephant; you get down from a duck.

If you count 20 houses on your right going to school, and 20 houses on your left coming home, how many houses in all have you counted?

Twenty. You counted the same houses going and coming.

How many months have 28 days?
All of them.

What animal walks on 4 feet in the morning, 2 at noon, and 3 in the evening?

Man. He goes on all fours as a baby, on two feet when he is grown, and uses a cane in old age.
(This is the oldest known riddle in the world. It was posed by the Sphinx in ancient Greek mythology and answered by Oedipus.)

Where does satisfaction come from?
From a satisfactory.

If you had a million dollars and gave away one quarter, and another quarter, and then another quarter, how much would you have left?

A million dollars minus 75 cents.

Some ducks were walking down a path. There was a duck in front of two ducks, a duck behind two ducks, and a duck between two ducks. How many ducks were there in all?

Three ducks, waddling single file.

What is very light but can't be lifted?
A bubble.

What doesn't exist but has a name?
Nothing.

How can you leave a room with two legs and return with six legs?
Bring a chair back with you.

A man started to town with a fox, a goose and a sack of corn. He came to a stream which he had to cross in a tiny boat. He could only take one across at a time. He could not leave the fox alone with the goose or the goose alone with the corn. How did he get them all safely over the stream?
He took the goose over first and came back. Then he took the fox across and brought the goose back. Next he took the corn over. He came back alone and took the goose.

151

What word can you pronounce quicker by adding a syllable to it?

Quick.

What is black when you buy it, red as you use it, and grey when you throw it out?

Coal.

Two fathers and two sons went duck hunting. Each shot a duck but they shot only three ducks in all. How come?

The hunters were a man, his son and his grandson.

What has 2 arms, 2 wings, 2 tails, 3 heads, 3 bodies and 8 legs?

A man on a horse holding a chicken.

What is filled every morning and emptied every night, except once a year when it is filled at night and emptied in the morning?

A stocking.

When the dog lover put his fingers in the dog's mouth to see how many teeth it had, what did the dog do?

The dog closed its mouth to see how many fingers the dog lover had.

What cannot be seen but only heard, and will not speak unless it is spoken to?

An echo.

Who is it that everybody listens to but nobody believes?

The weatherman.

What is easy to get into but hard to get out of?

Trouble.

What is pronounced like one letter, written with three letters, and belongs to all animals?

Eye.

Why do you always find something in the last place you look?

Because when you find it, you stop looking.

Why do we say "amen" and not "awomen?"

Because we sing "hymns," not "hers."

What grows larger the more you take away?

A hole.

What rises up in the morning and waves all day?

A flag.

Which two letters of the alphabet are nothing?
MT (empty).

What is the difference between the rising and the setting sun?
A day.

When is it good to lose your temper?
When you have a bad one.

What is always coming but never arrives?
Tomorrow.

What relation is a loaf of bread to a locomotive?
Mother. Bread is a necessity, a locomotive is an invention, and "Necessity is the mother of invention."

What is it that you can take away the whole and still have some left?
The word "wholesome."

What is heavier in warm weather than in winter?
Traffic to the beach.

How did rich people get their money?
They were calm and collected.

12 What Do You Want To Be When You Grow Up?

What did the invisible girl want to be when she grew up?

A gone-gone dancer.

What are doctors?

People who practice medicine but charge as if they know it.

What kind of doctor treats ducks?

A quack.

What is a thirsty physician?

A dry dock (doc).

What do you call the person who mows the grass of a baseball field?

A diamond cutter.

What did the laundry man say to the impatient customer?

"Keep your shirt on!"

What is the difference between a dressmaker and a farmer?

A dressmaker sews what she gathers, a farmer gathers what he sows.

What is the difference between a jeweler and a jailer?

A jeweler sells watches, a jailer watches cells.

Why did the spy pull the sheets over his head?

He was an undercover agent.

Why do people dislike going to the dentist?

Because he is boring.

Why was the banker bored?

Because he lost interest in everything.

What do you call an undertaker in the South?

A Southern planter.

How do undertakers speak?

Gravely.

Why is a shoemaker like a clergyman?

Both try to save soles (souls).

What do you call a minister named "Fiddle?"

Fiddle, D.D.

What person tries to make you smile most of the time?

A photographer.

Why was the photographer arrested?

Because he shot people and blew them up.

What did Cinderella say when her photos didn't show up?

"Some day my prints (prince) will come."

What is the difference between a tailor and a horse trainer?

One mends a tear, the other tends a mare.

Why is a drama teacher like the Pony Express?

Because he is a stage coach.

How is a judge like an English teacher?

They both hand out long sentences.

What does a farmer grow if he works hard enough?

Tired.

What do atomic scientists do when they go on vacation?

They go fission (fishing).

Who makes a million dollars a day?

Someone who works in a mint.

Why are twin doctors puzzling?

They are a paradox (pair of docs).

Who was the first nuclear scientist?

Eve because she knew all about the atom (Adam).

What kind of artist can't you trust?

A sculptor because he is always chiseling.

Why shouldn't you believe painters?
Because they spread it on thick.

What did the painter say to the wall?
"One more crack like that and I'll plaster you!"

How do you learn to work in an ice cream parlor?
You go to sundae (Sunday) school.

Why do misers talk so little?
Because they don't like to put their two cents in.

Why did the lazy man want to work in the bakery?
Because he was a loafer.

Why did the baker stop making doughnuts?
Because he got tired of the whole (hole) thing.

Why did the baker stop baking bread?
Because he wasn't making enough dough.

Why did the baker quit his job?
Because his work was so crummy (crumby).

What did the woman say to the adding machine?
"I'm counting on you."

What happens to a postman when he gets old?
He loses his zip.

Why was the cowboy a lot of laughs?
He was always horsing around.

What was Noah's profession?

He was an arkitect (architect).

What kind of a truck does a ballerina drive?

A toe (tow) truck.

What kind of car does an electrician drive?

A Volts Wagon (Volkswagen).

What kind of car does Dracula drive?

A bloodmobile.

What is an astronomer?

A night watchman with a college education.

For what person do all men take off their hats?

The barber.

If the Pilgrims came over on the Mayflower, how did the barbers arrive?

On clipper ships.

What kind of policemen enjoy their work most?

Traffic policemen, because they whistle while they work.

If you crossed a jeweler and a laundry man, what would you have?

Ring around the collar.

Why was Count Dracula glad to help young vampires?

He liked to see new blood in the business.

If you crossed a gangster and a garbage man, what would you have?

Organized grime (crime).

Why are garbage men unhappy?

Because they are down in the dumps so much.

Why did the woman who mended bowls go crazy?

She was around cracked pots (crackpots) too long.

What kind of job did the lazy man get?

He stood around so long doing nothing, he became a dust collector.

Why did the girl who worked for the telephone company sing all the time?

Because she was an operetta (operator).

What do you call the person who judges art contests?
An artificial (art official).

Who judges baking contests?
A pirate.

What profession did the parrot get into when it swallowed the clock?
Politics (Polly ticks).

What kind of ribbon do politicians use?
Red tape.

What did the rabbit want to be when he grew up?
He wanted to join the Hare (Air) Force.

What did the ghost want to do when he grew up?
He wanted to join the Ghost (Coast) Guard.

What did the worm want to do when he grew up?
He wanted to join the Apple Core (Corps).

Why was the Marine sergeant discharged?
Because he was rotten to the Corps (core).

When do mathematicians die?
When their numbers are up.

What do historians talk about when they meet?
Old times, of course.

What person helps bring up thousands of people?
The elevator operator.

What could you call a highly educated and skilled plumber?
A drain surgeon.

What key in music makes a good army officer?
A Sharp Major.

When does it pay to be boring?
When you're a ditch digger.

How do sailors get their clothes clean?
They throw them overboard and they wash ashore.

What is the difference between a blind man and a retired sailor?
The blind man cannot see to go, the retired sailor cannot go to sea.

What is an expert on soda pop?
A fizzician (physician).

What is the difference between a fisherman and a lazy student?

One baits his hook, the other hates his book.

What is the difference between a locomotive engineer and a teacher?

One minds the train, the other trains the mind.

Why did the cross-eyed teacher lose his job?

Because he couldn't control his pupils.

When is a teacher like a bird of prey?

When he watches you like a hawk.

Why did the pretty school teacher marry the janitor?

Because he swept her off her feet.

Why did the waiter stomp on his customer's hamburger?

Because the customer was in a hurry and told the waiter to step on it.

At what sports do waiters excel?

Tennis. They really know how to serve.

What did the little skunk want to be when it grew up?

A big stinker.

What nail doesn't a carpenter like to hit?

His fingernail.

Why are there no psychiatrists for dogs?
Everyone knows dogs aren't allowed on couches.

Why did the doctor keep his bandages in the refrigerator?
Because he wanted to use them for cold cuts.

What is a tailor's son?
A son of a so-and-so (sew-and-sew).

What do you have to know to be a real estate salesman?
Lots.

What person always falls down on the job?
A paratrooper.

What salesman has the slickest line?
A hair grease salesman.

What happened when the girl met the goat in the dairy?

The goat turned to butter (butt her).

What insect does a blacksmith make?

The firefly.

How do fish go into business?

They start on a small scale.

Why is a shoemaker's job unpleasant?

Because of all the lowdown heels that he has to work with.

At this moment everyone in the world is doing the same thing. What is it?

Getting older.

Why did the hippie become a coal miner?
Because he always said, "I dig."

What is the difference between a composer and a
letter carrier?
One writes notes, the other delivers them.

What is the difference between a gardener and a
billiard player?
One minds his peas, the other minds his cues.

What kind of job is it easy to stick to?
Working in a glue factory.

Why did the man like his work in the towel factory?
It was a very absorbing job.

How do they pay people who work in a candle factory?
By the wick (week).

Why didn't the girl go to work in the wool factory?
Because she was too young to dye (die).

Why was the worker fired from his job in the mattress
factory?
Because he was caught lying down on the job.

Why was the expert in the pretzel factory fired?
He tried to straighten things out.

13 Trouble Trouble Trouble

When things go wrong, what can you always count on?
Your fingers.

Why was the musician arrested?
He got into treble (trouble).

Why were screams coming from the kitchen?
The cook was beating the eggs.

Is it dangerous to swim on a full stomach?
Yes. It is better to swim in water.

Why is a banana peel on the sidewalk like music?
Because if you don't C sharp you'll B flat.

If you plug your electric blanket into the toaster, what happens?
You pop up all night.

For how long a period of time did Cain hate his brother?
As long as he was Abel (able).

What kind of spy hangs around department stores?
A counterspy.

What happened when the man sat on a pin?
Nothing. It was a safety pin.

Why did the spy speak in a whisper?
Because he was on a hush-hush mission.

What should a girl wear when she wants to end a fight?
Makeup.

Why is an eye like a man being flogged?
Because it's under the lash.

When do public speakers steal lumber?
When they take the floor.

What did the delicatessen sell after it burned down?
Smoked meats.

What three letters in the alphabet frighten criminals?
F.B.I.

What criminals can you find in a shoe store?
A pair of sneakers.

What diploma do criminals get?
The third degree.

When is a clock nervous?
When it is all wound up.

Why should a clock never be put upstairs?
It might run down and strike one.

Why do people beat their clocks?
To kill time.

A police officer had a brother, but the brother had no brother. How could this be?
The police officer was a woman.

Who were the the first gamblers?
Adam and Eve. They had a paradise (pair of dice).

How can you avoid falling hair?
Get out of the way.

Spell mousetrap with three letters.
C-A-T.

Why wasn't the girl afraid of the shark?
Because it was a man-eating shark.

Why is a dictionary dangerous?
Because it has "dynamite" in it.

A policeman saw a truck driver going the wrong way down a one-way street, but didn't give him a ticket. Why not?
The truck driver was walking.

Why did the dragon swallow the pesty knight?
Because he was a pill.

If you were walking in a jungle and saw a lion, what time would it be?

Time to run.

Why shouldn't you grab a tiger by his tail?

It may only be his tail, but it could be your end.

If an African lion fought an African tiger, who would win?

Neither. There are no tigers in Africa.

Why does a dog chasing a rabbit resemble a bald-headed man?

He makes a little hare (hair) go a long way.

What would you have if your car's motor was in flames?

A fire engine.

What ghost haunted the King of England in 18th century?

The Spirit of '76.

What did the rug say to the floor?

"I've got you covered."

What did the picture say to the wall?

"I've been framed."

What did the paintbrush say to the floor?

"One more word and I'll shellac you!"

What did the cork say to the bottle?

"If you don't behave yourself, I'll plug you."

What did one cucumber say to the other cucumber?

"If you kept your big mouth shut, we wouldn't be in this pickle."

Why did the hens refuse to lay any more eggs?

Because they were tired of working for chicken feed.

What would happen if black widow spiders were as big as horses?

If one bit you, you could ride it to the hospital.

What Indian goes to court?

A Sioux (sue) Indian.

What kind of clothes do lawyers wear?
Lawsuits.

Where is the best place to hide a lawyer?
In a brief case.

When did the criminal get smart?
When the judge threw the book at him.

Why is your heart like a policeman?
Because it follows a regular beat.

Why can't you keep secrets in a bank?
Because of all the tellers.

Can you spell jealousy with two letters?
NV (envy).

What happens if an ax falls on your car?
You have an ax-i-dent (accident).

What kind of soldier doesn't need bullets?
A soldier who is always shooting his mouth off.

When is an army totally destroyed?
When it is in quarters.

What is in the army and is corny?
A colonel (kernel).

Why did the kid punch the bed?
His mother told him to hit the hay.

Why did the cowboy get a hot seat?
Because he rode the range.

Why was the lobster arrested?
Because he was always pinching things.

Why did the sheriff arrest the tree?
Because its leaves rustled.

Why was the skunk arrested for counterfeiting?
Because he gave out bad scents (cents).

Why was the dirty kid arrested?
For grime (crime).

Why were the tennis players arrested?
Because they were involved with racquets (rackets).

How did the chimpanzee escape from his cage?
He used a monkey wrench.

What bird always runs from a fight?
A canary, because it is yellow.

Why are farmers cruel?
Because they pull corn by the ears.

What is a hangman's favorite reading material?
A noosepaper (newspaper).

What did the kangaroo say when her baby was missing?
"Help! My pocket's been picked."

What is big and white and is found in Florida?
A lost polar bear.

Why couldn't the clock be kept in jail?
Because time was always running out.

What kind of robbery is not dangerous?
A safe robbery.

Did you hear about the holdup in the yard?
Two clothespins held up a pair of pants.

What kind of Indians does Dracula like?
Full-blooded ones.

What do you call a man when a Marine sits on him?
A submarine.

Why is it confusing when a dog growls and wags his tail at the same time?
It's hard to know which end to believe.

What is a very hair-raising experience?
Visiting a rabbit farm.

What letter should you avoid?
The letter A because it makes men mean.

How can you jump off a 50-foot ladder without getting hurt?
Jump off the bottom rung.

What is a frozen policeman?
A copsicle.

If five boys beat up one boy, what time would it be?
Five to one.

If you were surrounded by 10 lions, 4 tigers, 3 grizzly bears and 4 leopards, how could you escape?
Wait until the merry-go-round stops and get off.

Why did the outlaw carry a bottle of glue when he went to rob the stagecoach?
He wanted to stick up the passengers.

People's houses have rooms. What does Dracula's house have?
Glooms.

Why did the chicken run away from home?
Because she was tired of being cooped up.

How do you spell a hated opponent with three letters?
NME (enemy).

Why did the dog run away from home?
Doggone if I know!

Why is a sinking ship like a person in jail?
Because it needs bailing out.

Why did the robber take a bath?
So he could make a clean getaway.

What kind of puzzle makes people angry?
A crossword puzzle.

How can you tell when a mummy is angry?
When he flips his lid.

What happened when the chimney got angry?
It blew its stack.

Why was the lady's hair angry?
Because she was always teasing it.

Why is the ocean angry?
Because it has been crossed so many times.

Why is a thief like a thermometer on a hot day?

Because they are both up to something.

What is the difference between a thief and a church bell?

One steals from the people, the other peals from the steeple.

Why does Father Time wear bandages?

Because day breaks and night falls.

What did one skunk say to the other skunk when they were cornered?

"Let us spray."

What weapon is most feared by knights?

A can opener.

What is a torpedo?

A seashell (sea shell).

What is a rifle with three barrels?

A trifle.

When do ghosts have to stop scaring people?

When they lose their haunting (hunting) licenses.

Why is it hard to steal pigs?
Because pigs are squealers.

What animal breaks the law?
A cheetah.

What animal has a chip on its shoulder?
A chipmunk.

What is a skunk's best defense against enemies?
Instinct.

If you cross a lion and a mouse, what will you have?
A mighty mouse.

How can you come face-to-face with a hungry, angry
lion, dare him to fight, and still be unafraid?
Walk calmly to the next cage.

Why was the insect kicked out of the forest?
Because it was a litterbug.

What did one clock say to the other clock when it
was frightened?
"Don't be alarmed."

What did the coward say to the stamp?
"I bet I can lick you."

What did the leopard say when he swallowed the man?
"That hit the spot!"

What was the most dangerous time for knights?
Nightfall (knight fall).

Which is better: "The house burned *down*" or "The house burned up?"
Neither. They are both bad.

What do you call a worn-out rifle?
A shotgun (shot gun).

What would you get if Batman and Robin were run over by a herd of stampeding elephants?
Flatman and Ribbon.

How does an octopus go to war?
Armed.

Why is law like the ocean?
Because most trouble is caused by the breakers.

14 Winners & Losers

How do chickens start a race?
From scratch.

What is a fast duck?
A quick quack.

Why did the orange stop in the middle of the road?
It ran out of juice.

A lemon and an orange were on a high diving board.
The orange jumped off. Why didn't the lemon?
Because it was yellow.

Why did they throw the elephants out of the swimming
pool?
Because they couldn't hold their trunks up.

If you were swimming in the ocean and a big
alligator attacked you, what should you do?
Nothing. There are no alligators in the ocean.

Why shouldn't you tell a joke while you are ice
skating?
Because the ice might crack up.

Why don't sheep have much money?
Because they're always getting fleeced.

Why did the kangaroo mother scold her child?
For eating crackers in bed.

Why wasn't the elephant allowed on the airplane?
Because his trunk was too big to fit under the seat.

What kind of party do prisoners in jail like most of all.
A going-away party.

When do clocks die?
When their time is up.

What game can be dangerous to your mental health?
Marbles, if you lose them.

What stars go to jail?
Shooting stars.

What did the bee say to the rose?
"Hi Bud!"

What did the rose answer?
"Buzz off!"

What did the blackbird say to the scarecrow?
"I can beat the stuffing out of you!"

What did one grape say to the other grape?
"If it wasn't for you, we wouldn't be in this jam."

Why is someone who borrows money but does not pay it all back like a football player?

Because sometimes he gives you a quarter back and sometimes a half back.

Why are jackasses good football players?

Because when they kick they seldom miss.

Two baseball teams played a game. One team won but no man touched base. How could that be?

Both were all-girl teams.

Why was Cinderella thrown off the baseball team?

Because she ran away from the ball.

What team cries when it loses?

A bawl club.

What is the difference between an ice cream cone and a bully?

You lick one, the other licks you.

Two men were playing checkers. They played five games, and each man won the same number of games. How is that possible?

They played different people.

When it rains cats and dogs, what do you step into?

Poodles.

What did the frankfurter say when the dog bit him?

"It's a dog-eat-dog world."

What line do children stand on to use the wading pool?

A wading (waiting) line.

How is a ghost child taught to count to ten?

One, boo, three, four, five, six, seven, hate, nine, frighten.

What did the yacht say to the dock?
"Yacht's (what's) up, Doc?"

What did the pitcher say to the cup?
"I'll have none of your lip."

When is it bad luck to have a black cat follow you?
When you are a mouse.

What is a person who steals Honda bikes?
A Honda-taker (undertaker).

What do you get if your sheep studies karate?
A lamb chop.

What kind of skates wear out quickly?
Cheapskates (cheap skates).

How do fireflies start a race?
When someone says, "Ready, set, glow!"

What is the best way to win a race?
Run faster than anybody else.

Why do you run faster when you have a cold?
You have a racing pulse and a running nose.

If George Washington were alive today, why couldn't
he throw a silver dollar across the Potomac?
Because a dollar doesn't go as far as it used to.

What kind of sandwich speaks for itself?
A tongue sandwich.

Why is an airline pilot like a football player?
They both want to make safe touchdowns.

Who are the happiest people at the football game?
The cheer leaders.

What color is a cheerleader?
Yeller (yellow).

If your watch is broken, why can't you go fishing?
Because you don't have the time.

What is the best way to communicate with a fish?
Drop him a line.

What did one fish say to the other?
"If you keep your big mouth shut, you won't get caught."

What game do girls dislike?
Soccer (sock her).

What famous prize do cats win?
The A-cat-emy (Academy) Award.

What dog has money?
A bloodhound, because he is always picking up scents (cents).

What kind of dog hangs around bowling alleys?
A setter.

Why are dogs experts on trees?
They have to be if they don't want to bark up the wrong one.

If you're crazy about chess, why should you keep away from squirrels?
Because squirrels eat chestnuts (chess nuts).

What is the best advice to give a young baseball player?
If you don't succeed at first, try second base.

Which takes longer to run: from first to second base or from second to third base?

From second to third base, because there is a shortstop in the middle.

Where does Superman get the kind of food he needs to make him strong?

At the supermarket.

Why did the team sign a two-headed baseball player?

To play the double-headers.

A dog was tied to a 15-foot rope, but he walked 30 feet. How come?

The rope wasn't tied to anything.

What did the dog say when it was scratched by the cat?

Nothing. Dogs can't talk.

What is a cold war?

A snowball fight.

Why did the rooster refuse to fight?

Because he was chicken.

Why are mountain climbers curious?

They always want to take another peak (peek).

What goes 99-thump, 99-thump, 99-thump?
A centipede with a wooden leg.

What is a stupid mummy?
A dummy mummy.

Why did the mummy leave his tomb after 2,000 years?
He thought he was old enough to leave home.

Which will burn longer: the candles on the birthday cake of a boy, or the candles on the birthday cake of a girl?
Neither. No candles burn longer. They all burn shorter.

What happens to old horses?
They become nags.

Why do turkeys eat so little?
Because they are always stuffed.

Why were the elephants the last animals to leave the ark?
They had to pack their trunks.

What is a sorcerer who casts only good spells?
A charming fellow.

Why shouldn't you listen to people who have just come out of the swimming pool?
Because they are all wet.

When can you jump over three men without getting up?

In a checker game.

What kind of bell doesn't ring?

A dumbbell.

August was the name of a puppy who was always picking on larger animals. One day he got into an argument with a lion. The next day was the first day of September. Why?

Because that was the last of August.

Why do ducks look so sad?

When they preen their feathers, they get down in the mouth.

What kind of policeman dresses poorly?

A plain clothesman.

Why are birds poor?

Because money doesn't grow on trees.

What drives a baseball batter crazy?

A pitcher who throws screwballs.

Why is a scrambled egg like a losing ball team?

Because both are beaten.

Why was the mummy sent into the game as a pinchhitter?

With a mummy at bat, the game would be all wrapped up.

Why did the silly couple want to get married in the bathtub?

They wanted a double-ring ceremony.

Why are shaggy dogs useful to have around the house?

Roll them around the floor and you have a good dust mop.

Why couldn't the dog catch his tail?

Because it is hard to make ends meet these days.

Why aren't horses well dressed?

Because they wear shoes but no socks.

Why didn't horses like Theodore Roosevelt?

Because he was a rough rider.

What is the best exercise for losing weight?

Pushing yourself away from the table.

What do ants use for hula hoops?
Cheerios.

What kind of insect likes to bowl?
A boll weevil.

Why do good bowlers play so slowly?
Because they have time to spare.

Why was the skeleton a coward?
Because he had no guts.

Why do skeletons drink a lot of milk?
Because it is good for the bones.

Why did the wife understand her invisible husband so well?
Because she could see right through him.

If Fortune had a daughter. what would her name be?
Misfortune (Miss Fortune).

What is a stupid ant?
An ignorant.

What did the bow tie say to the boy?
"You double-crossed me."

What did the stove say to the pot?
"I can make things hot for you."

What did the window say to the Venetian blind?
"If it weren't for you, it would be curtains for me."

Why are lollipops like racehorses?
The more you lick them the faster they go.

How can you make a slow horse fast?
Don't give him any food.

What did one horse say to the other horse?
"I forget your name but your pace (face) is familiar."

Why did the stale girl loaf of bread slap the stale boy loaf of bread?
Because he tried to get fresh.

Women don't have it and don't want it. Men get it, think it's a good thing but they often try to get rid of it. What is it?
A beard.

What insect lives on nothing?

A moth because it eats holes.

Why did the bald man put a rabbit on his head?

Because he wanted a head of hare (hair).

Why was Adam known to be a good runner?

He was the first in the human race.

If two people had a race and one had sand in his shoe but the other did not, who would win?

The one with the sand in his shoe—if it was quicksand.

A cabbage, a faucet and a tomato had a race. How did it go?

The cabbage was ahead, the faucet was running, and the tomato tried to ketchup.

What is the proper way to address the king of the ghosts?

"Your ghostliness."

Why couldn't the mountain climber call for help?

Because he was hanging by his teeth.

Why are owls brave?

Because they don't give a hoot about anything.

What happened to the sardine when it didn't show up for work?

It was canned.

15 Oh, No!

What would you call two bananas?
A pair of slippers.

What would you call the life story of a car?
An autobiography.

What do you get if you hit a
counterfeit penny with a
hatchet?
A phony accent (ax cent).

What do you call a hippie's wife?
Mississippi (Mrs. Hippie).

What part of a clock is always
old?
The second hand.

What do you get if you cross a
squirrel and a kangaroo?
*An animal that carries
nuts in its pocket.*

What is a banged-up used car?
A car in first-crash condition.

What does Santa Claus do when it is not Christmas?
*He is probably a farmer because he always says,
"Hoe, hoe, hoe!"*

Why is a book like a king?
Because they both have pages.

Why shouldn't you believe a father goose?
*Because anything he might say is pappaganda
(propaganda).*

What is black and white and red all over?
A newspaper.

What is black and white and red all over?
A sunburned zebra.

What is black and white and red all over?
A skunk with diaper rash.

What is black and white and red all over?
A blushing penguin.

What is the correct height for people to stand?
Over two feet.

What does a dog get when it graduates from dog school?
A pedigree.

What is the difference between a dog and a flea?
A dog can have fleas but a flea can't have dogs.

What kind of truck is always a "he" and never a "she?"
A mail (male) truck.

Why are men going bald at an older age these days?
Because they're wearing their hair longer.

Who invented the telephone?
The Phoenicians (phone-itions).

What are the most faithful insects?
Ticks. Once they find friends, they stick to them.

What would happen if you swallowed your knife and fork?
You would have to eat with your hands.

If a papa bull eats three bales of hay and a baby bull eats one bale, how much hay will a mama bull eat?
Nothing. There is no such thing as a mama bull.

What should you do when you find Chicago, Ill.?
Call Baltimore, M.D.

Where can you always find diamonds?
In a deck of cards.

Why do statues and paintings of George Washington always show him standing?
Because he would never lie.

What causes baldness?
Lack of hair.

What animals are well educated?
Fish, because they go around in schools.

What Spanish name opens the Star Spangled Banner?
José ("Oh, say can you see?")

What is an ocean?
Where buoy meets gull (boy meets girl).

Why shouldn't you carry two half dollars in your pocket?
Because two halves make a whole (hole), and you could lose your money.

What is green and pecks on trees?
Woody Wood Pickle.

What is a parasite?
Something you see in Paris.

What happened when Frankenstein met a girl monster?

They fell in love at first fright.

What did the boy Frankenstein say to the girl Frankenstein?

"You are so electrocute."

How can you tell if a ghost is about to faint?

He gets pale as a sheet.

What did one invisible man say to the other invisible man?

"It's nice not to see you again."

What do you call someone who carries a dictionary in his jeans?

Smarty pants.

When is an army like a sales clerk making out a bill?
When it is ready to charge.

Why did the three little pigs leave home?
Because their father was a big boar (bore).

Why do cats sleep better in summer than in winter?
Because summer brings the caterpillar (cat a pillow).

Why did the girl sit on her watch?
She wanted to be on time.

What 8-letter word has one letter in it?
Envelope.

What are the three swiftest means of communication?
Telephone, telegraph and tell-a-secret.

What is an ultimate?
The last person you marry.

"Did you hear the story about the smog?"
"You don't have to tell me, it's all over town."

What is big and purple and lies in the sea?
Grape Britain.

What is a ship for good writers?
Penmanship.

What is the front part of a geography book?
The table of continents (contents).

What did one car say to the other?
"You look familiar. Haven't we bumped into each other before?"

What two words have thousands of letters in them?
Post office.

When do princes become kings?
Mostly in April, when the rains (reigns) begin.

Why do hurricanes travel so fast?
Because if they travelled slowly, we'd have to call them slow-*i*-canes.

If fish lived on land, where would they live?
In Finland.

If two's company and three's a crowd, what is four and five?
Nine.

How can you eat and study at the same time?
Eat alphabet soup.

Why are Boy Scouts chubby?
Because scouting rounds a guy out.

What does a farmer call a steer that he borrows and has to return?
A stereo (steer he owe).

When are people smartest?
During the day, because when the sun shines everything is brighter.

What did the little calf say to the haystack?
"Are you my fodder (father)?"

How do you buy things in Mexico?
The same way you buy things anywhere else. You peso (pay so) much and you buy it.

Why are we sure that Indians were the first people in North America?
Because they had reservations.

What did one magnet say to the other magnet?
"I find you very attractive."

What did one faucet say to the other faucet?
"You're a big drip."

What did one insect say to the other insect?
"Stop bugging me."

What happens to tires when they get old?
They are retired.

What animal is gray and has a trunk?
A mouse going on vacation.

What did the stocking with the hole say to the shoe?
"Well, I'll be darned!"

What did the necktie say to the hat?
"You go on ahead. I'll hang around for a while."

If there were no food left, what could people do?
Country people could eat their forest preserves and city people could have their traffic jams.

Why do people laugh up their sleeves?
That's where their funny bones are.

Why did the man keep a ruler on his newspaper?
Because he wanted to get the story straight.

Why can you always believe a ruler?
Because it is on the level.

Why did the boy take the ruler to bed?
He wanted to see how long he slept.

Where does Friday come before Thursday?
In the dictionary.

What did the wig say to the head?
"I've got you covered."

If the green house is on the right side of the road, and the red house is on the left side of the road, where is the white house?
In Washington, D.C.

What letter stands for the ocean?
The letter C.

Why did the boy put his head in the washing machine?

He wanted to have that "wet look."

Why did the boy put his head in the dryer?

Because he wanted to have that "dry look."

Where can you find cards on a ship?

On the deck.

What radio has a crewcut?

A short-wave radio.

How do they drink water in the South?

From Dixie cups.

Where do taxis go when you trade them in?

To the old cabbage (cab age) home.

What did the big carburetor say to the little carburetor?

"Don't inhale so fast or you'll choke."

What did one windshield wiper say to the other windshield wiper?

"Isn't it a shame we seem to meet only when it rains?"

How can you say rabbit without using the letter R?

Bunny.

Why did the girl put sugar under her pillow?

She wanted sweet dreams.

What do hill people use to cook their food on?
A mountain range.

Who takes longer to get ready for a trip—an elephant or a rooster?
The elephant. He has to pack a trunk while the rooster only takes his comb.

What is a ringleader?
The first person in the bathtub.

When do the leaves begin to turn?
The night before a test.

When do your car's brakes work best?
In the morning when its breakfast (brake fast) time.

How can you get out of a locked room with a piano in it?
Play the piano until you find the right key and you can get out.

What happens when two oxen bump into each other?
You have an oxident (accident).

Why were the inventors of the airplane correct in thinking they could fly?
Because they were Wright (right).

Why do scientists look for things twice?
Because they research (re-search) everything.

What person can jump higher than a house?

Anyone. A house can't jump.

What is the difference between a man and a running dog?

One wears trousers, the other pants.

What kind of clothing does a pet dog wear?

A petticoat.

What did the shirt say to the pants?

"Meet me at the clothesline. That's where I hang out."

What kind of story is the story about the three little pigs?

A pigtail (pig tale).

What did the book say to the librarian?

"Can I take you out?"

What did one girl calendar say to the other girl calendar?

"I have more dates than you do."

Why did the girl tear the calendar?

Because she wanted to take a month off.

What is a dentist's office?

A filling station.

What would happen if you ate yeast and polish?

You would rise and shine.

16 Far Out

What do you do with a green monster?
Wait till he ripens.

What sits on the bottom of the sea and shakes?
A nervous wreck.

What is a witch doctor's mistake?
A voodoo boo-boo.

What kind of jokes did Einstein make?
Wisecracks.

At what time of day was Adam born?
A little before Eve.

What is long and yellow and always points north?
A magnetic banana.

Why did the athlete blink his eyelashes all day?
He needed batting practice.

What did the little kid do with the dead battery?
He buried it.

Why did the mad chef throw the chicken off the balcony?

Because he wanted to make egg drop soup.

What occurs once in every minute twice in every moment, but not once in a thousand years?

The letter M.

What are the six main seasons?

Summer, fall, winter, spring, salt and pepper.

What is a locomotive?

A crazy reason for doing something.

Where does a liar sleep?

In a bunk bed.

Which astronaut wears the biggest helmet?
The one with the biggest head.

What does an astronaut do when he gets angry?
He blasts off.

What do people do in a clock factory?
They make faces all day.

What do you call a person who looks over your shoulder while you are eating at the lunch counter?
A counterspy.

What is purple and conquered the world?
Alexander the Grape.

What travels around the world but stays in a corner?
A stamp.

What do you have if you cross a witch and a millionaire?
A witch (rich) person.

What would you get if you crossed a skunk and an eagle?
An animal that stunk to high heaven.

How can you make varnish disappear?
Take out the R.

Is a unicorn male or female?
Female. The unicorn is a myth (Miss).

What time is it when a knight looks at his belly button?
It is the middle of the night (knight).

Why did the horses go on strike?
To get more horsepower.

Whose cow talks Russian?
Ma's cow (Moscow).

Why did the cowboy's car stop?
It had Injun (engine) trouble.

What did the explorer say when he saw the Pacific Ocean for the first time?
"Long time no see (sea)."

Are you crazy if you talk to yourself?
Not unless you answer.

What is the difference between a counterfeit dollar and a crazy rabbit?
One is bad money, the other is a mad bunny.

What is the difference between a cloud and a spanked child?
One pours down rain, the other roars with pain.

In what school do you have to drop out in order to graduate?
Parachute school.

If you cross a lion and a monkey, what do you have?
A swinging lion.

If you cross a camera and a mirror, what do you get?
A camera that takes pictures of itself.

What do you get if you cross a jumbo jet and a kangaroo?
A plane that makes short hops.

What would you get if you crossed a pigeon, a frog, and a prehistoric monster?
A pigeon-toed (toad) dinosaur.

What do you get when you cross a lion and a parrot?
I don't know, but if it wants a cracker, you'd better give it one.

Why did it take three husky Boy Scouts to help the little old lady cross the street?

Because she didn't want to go.

What do you call an ocean plantation?

A pharmacy (farm-asea).

What holds the moon up?

Moonbeams.

Why is a grape religious?

Because it comes from divine (the vine).

Where do good pigs go when they die?

To a sty in the sky.

What did one angel say to the other angel?

"Halo."

What kind of clothes did Cinderella wear?

Wish and wear clothes.

Why does the Statue of Liberty stand?
Because she can't sit down.

If a millionaire sits on his gold, who sits on silver?
The Lone Ranger.

Why did the pirate put a chicken where he buried his treasure?
Because eggs (X) marks the spot.

Why did the one-eyed chicken cross the road?
Because there was a Bird's Eye factory across the street.

Why did the chicken cross the road twice?
Because she was a double-crosser.

Why did the chicken go just halfway across the road?
She wanted to lay it on the line.

Why did the chicken cross the road?
With traffic the way it is today, probably to commit suicide.

What happened to Humpty Dumpty after he had a great fall?
He was made into an egg salad sandwich for all the king's men.

Why did Humpty Dumpty have a great fall?
To make up for a bad summer.

What would you have if a young goat fell into a blender?

A mixed-up kid.

Why doesn't Saint Nicholas shave?

Every time he tries, he nicks himself.

What kind of salads do hippies like?

Tossed salads because they are all shook up.

How many balls of string would it take to reach the moon?

One, if it were long enough.

Why won't people ever go to the moon for their vacation?

Because it lacks atmosphere.

What kind of insects live on the moon?

Lunatics (lunar ticks).

Why are false teeth like stars?

Because they come out at night.

What person watches the stars?

A movie fan.

What did the stamp say to the envelope?

"I've become attached to you."

What did the envelope say to the stamp?

"Stick with me and we'll go places."

One day a man met three beggars. To the first he gave a dime, to the second a dime, and to the third a nickel. What time was it?

A quarter to three.

When do monster mothers receive gifts?

On Mummy's Day.

What kind of clock is crazy?

A cuckoo clock.

What has four eyes but can't see?

The Mississippi.

Why did the hippie like to stand in front of the electric fan?

It blew his mind.

How do you make an elephant float?
Take two scoops of ice cream, root beer, and add one elephant.

Why was the kid called "candy bar?"
Because he was half nuts.

Who is the most truthful man in Spain?
A bull fighter.

What dish is out of this world?
A flying saucer.

How can you get a cow into a frying pan?
Use shortening.

Is Ghostland a state?
No, it's a terror-tory (territory).

What weighs a thousand pounds, has four legs, flies, and is yellow?

Two five-hundred pound canaries.

How far can you go into a forest?

Only halfway—after that you would be coming out.

What is the end of everything?

The letter G.

Why is writing called handwriting?

If people wrote with their feet, we would have to call it footwriting.

What did people say when the man got out of his rocking chair after 20 years?

"He must be off his rocker."

What is yellow and swims underwater?

A yellow submarine.

Which has more legs, a horse or no horse?

No horse. A horse has four legs but no *horse has six legs.*

Why can't you hit a stove a mile away?

Because it is out of range.

What goes up and never comes down?

Your age.

What did one angel say to the other?
"What's harpening (happening)?"

Why did the old angel die?
He had a harp (heart) attack.

How do Iranians speak on the telephone?
Persian-to-Persian (person-to-person).

Why did the man buy a set of tools?
Everyone said he had a screw loose.

What did the boy vampire say to the girl vampire?
"I like your blood type."

What did the girl battery say to the boy battery?
"I get a big charge out of you."

What did the boy accordion say to the girl accordion?
"Every time I squeeze you I hear music."

What did the girl volcano say to the boy volcano?
"Do you lava (love) me like I lava you?"

What goes on in a planetarium?
An all-star show.

What colors would you paint the sun and the wind?
The sun rose and the wind blue (blew).

Where do flowers come from?
The stalk (stork) brings them.

Why did the girl stand on a ladder when she learned how to sing?

Because she wanted to reach the high notes.

Why did the man climb up to the chandelier?

He was a light sleeper.

What is big and red and eats rocks?

A big red rock eater.

What is the best year for a kangaroo?

Leap year.

When do you get that run-down feeling?

When a car hits you.

When does a river flood?

When it gets too big for its bridges (britches).

What is as annoying as a roaring river?
A babbling brook.

What is yellow, soft, and goes round and round?
A long-playing omelette.

What happens to an author after he dies?
He becomes a ghost writer.

Why did the invisible man go crazy?
Out of sight, out of mind.

Why did the kid cut a hole in the top of his umbrella?
So he could see when it stopped raining.

What is the difference between the North Pole and the South Pole?
The whole world.

What did the balloon say to the pin?
"Hi ya, Buster!"

What did one IBM card say to the other?
"I'm holier than you."

What did the fireman say when the church caught
on fire?
"Holy smoke!"

What kind of cats live in churches?
Holy cats!

Why did the absentminded professor put glue on his
head?
*Because he thought it would help things stick in
his mind.*

What trees do fortune tellers look at?
Palms.

What should you do with old fingernails?
File them.

What did the little kid answer when the teacher said,
"Order, children, order!"?
"I'll have a hamburger with ketchup."

Why is school out at three o'clock?
*The bell strikes one, strikes two, strikes three—
and you are out!*

What is a sleeping child?
A kidnapper.

What is a very popular perfume?
A best smeller.

Where does afternoon always come before morning?
In the dictionary.

When are people like eyeglasses?
When they make spectacles of themselves.

Why did the man put his car in the oven?
Because he wanted a hot rod.

What did the man put on his car when the weather was cold?
An extra muffler.

Why did the boy jump up and down on the letter?
He heard that you have to stamp letters or the post office won't send them.

If you cross a dog and a cat, what do you get?
An animal that chases itself.

17 Weird Characters

Why did the musician strike the phonograph record with a hammer?

He wanted a hit record.

What did the woodchopper do when he didn't know the time?

He axed (asked) someone.

If a girl ate her mother and father, what would that make her?

An orphan.

What is Frankenstein's favorite waterway?

The Erie (eerie) Canal.

Why did the dog run around in circles?

Because he was a watchdog and wanted to wind himself up.

Why was the puppy fat?

Because he always had a second yelping (helping).

What did the vegetable say when it was wrapped for another day?

"Curses, foiled again!"

What did Sir Lancelot wear to bed?

A nightgown (knight gown).

What does a two-hundred-pound mouse say?

"Here, Kitty, Kitty."

Why do elephants paint their toenails red?

So that they can hide in the strawberry patch.

Why do elephants wear green nail polish?

So they can hide in the pea patch.

Where does Frankenstein's wife have her hair done?

At the ugly parlor.

Who was the first swinger?

Tarzan.

What is green and flies?
Super Pickle.

Why does Batman brush his teeth at least three times
a day?
To prevent bat (bad) breath.

What general had a shocking personality?
General Electric.

What famous Greek might have invented baseball?
Homer.

What is an Italian referee?
A Roman umpire.

Who was the poet of basketball?
Longfellow.

Why did the hippie paint the landscape?
Because he wanted to make the scene.

If you cross a pig and a young goat, what do you
get?
A dirty kid.

What do you get if you cross a porcupine and a
young goat?
A stuck-up kid.

What gives milk and says, "Oom, oom?"
A cow walking backwards.

What is a clumsy Santa Claus?
A Santa Klutz.

What kind of boats do vampires take when they travel?
Blood vessels.

Why did the rabbit wear a shower cap?
Because he didn't want his hare (hair) to get wet.

Why did the kid roll rocks down the hill?
He wanted to see the Rolling Stones.

What branch of the army do babies join?
The infantry.

What would you call a knight caught in a windstorm?
A nightingale (knight in gale).

Why did the pig act up?
Because he was a big ham.

Chief Running Water had two sons. What were their names?
Hot and Cold.

Why did the astronomer hit himself on the head in the afternoon?
He wanted to see stars during the day.

What was Batman doing in the tree?
Looking for Robin's nest.

What kind of crew does a monster ship have?
A skeleton crew.

Why did the elephant swallow a camphor ball?
To keep moths out of his trunk.

Why did the farmer feed his cow money?
He wanted rich milk.

Why did the potato farmer use a steam roller?
Because he wanted to grow mashed potatoes.

Why did the mad chef watch the lazy cow?
He liked to see the meat loaf.

Why did the secretary ask for a round envelope?
Because she wanted to mail a circular.

Why didn't Count Dracula get married?
Because he was a bat-chelor (bachelor).

Why did the nasty kid put ice cubes in his aunt's bed?

Because he wanted to make antifreeze.

Why did the girl aim a cannon at the peas?

Because her mother told her to shell them.

What animal eats and drinks with its tail?

All do. No animal takes off his tail when eating or drinking.

What is the difference between a baseball player and a crazy pilot?

One bats flies, the other flies bats.

Why do you get a charge out of reading the newspaper?

Because it is full of current events.

What did the boots say to the cowboy?

"You ride, I'll go on foot."

What did the kid say when the dentist asked him what kind of filling he wanted?

"Chocolate."

Why did the playboy roll up the carpet?

He wanted to see the whole floor show.

What did the invisible kid want to be when he grew up?

A hippie, because then he would really be out of sight.

What did the invisible salesman say?

"What you don't see is what you don't get."

Why are story tellers strange?

Because tales (tails) come out of their heads.

Why did the girl put her bed in the fireplace?

So that she could sleep like a log.

Why did the boy run down the block with a clock in his pocket?

He wanted to keep up with the times.

Why did the butcher put bells on his scale?

Because he wanted the bells to jingle all the way (weigh).

What has 18 legs and catches flies?
A baseball team.

What is a baseball dog?
A dog that wears a muzzle, catches flies, chases fowls, and beats it for home when he sees the catcher.

Why did the fan bring a rope to the ball game?
So he could tie up the score.

What kind of person plays basketball with a shirt and tie?
A gym dandy.

Why did the man put his pants on backwards?
Because he didn't know whether he was coming or going.

Why do witches ride brooms?
Because vacuum cleaners are too hard to fly.

What kind of deer lives in a can?
A cantaloupe.

Why did King Kong play with the flying saucer?
He thought it was a frisbee.

Why did the girl keep running around her bed?
She wanted to catch up on her sleep.

Why did the writer put his fingers in the alphabet soup?

He was trying to find the right words.

Why did the banker keep looking up at the sky?
To see if there was any change in the weather.

What did the Martian say when he landed in the flower bed?

"Take me to your weeder (leader)."

What did the chick say when the hen sat on an orange?

"Look at the orange marmalade (mamma laid)."

What did the man say when he found that he was growing bald?

"Hair today and gone tomorrow!"

Why did the golfer wear two pairs of pants?
Just in case he got a hole in one.

How would you describe the expression on a zombie's face?
Deadpan.

Do zombies like being dead?
Of corpse! (Of course!)

Why did the lady jump in the ocean?
To get a wave in her hair.

What does an umpire do before he eats?
He brushes off his plate.

What is a crazy duck?
A wacky quacky.

Why does William live on a mountain?
Because he is a hillbilly.

What would you call a female Indian chief who is always getting into trouble?
Mischief.

Why did the timid soul always take cold baths?
Because he didn't want to get into hot water.

Why did the hippie only draw circles?
Because he didn't like squares.

What did one bird say to another as he saw a jet fly by?
"I bet I could fly that fast if my tail were on fire."

What did the pig say when the butcher grabbed him by the tail?
"That's the end of me!"

What did the 2,000-year-old boy say when he was dug up?
"I want my mummy!"

Why couldn't the mummy answer the telephone?
Because he was all tied up.

Who was the first man in space?
The man in the moon.

Why does an Indian wear feathers?
To keep his wigwam (wig warm).

Why did the baby goose think the car was its mother?

Because the car honked.

What is a doughnut?

A person who is crazy about money.

Why did the girl wear loud socks?

She didn't want her feet to fall asleep.

Why did the shoemaker's son try to put boots on the flies?

Because his father told him to shoo (shoe) them.

Why did the old man put wheels on his rocking chair?

Because he wanted to rock and roll.

What happened to Ray when he jumped off the Empire State Building?

He is now called X-ray.

What was the chicken with poor eyesight doing in the garden?

Sitting on an eggplant.

Why did the pelican put his leg in his mouth when he ate out?

He wanted to foot the bill.

18 Don't Look at These!

What do you call Eskimo cows?
Eskimoos.

What do you get if you cross a centipede and a parrot?
A walkie-talkie.

What do you get if you cross a chick and a guitar?
A chicken that makes music when you pluck it.

What do you get if you cross a homing pigeon and a woodpecker?
A bird that not only delivers messages, but also knocks on the door.

What do you get if you cross a cocker spaniel, a poodle and a rooster?
A cockapoodledoo.

What do you get if you cross a canary and a tiger?
I don't know, but when it sings you'd better listen.

What do two oceans say when they meet?
They don't say anything, they just wave.

What is the best way to pitch a tent?
It depends—sometimes overhand and sometimes underhand.

What nationality is Santa Claus?
North Polish.

What is long and thin and goes, "Hith, Hith?"
A snake with a lisp.

If a buttercup is yellow, what color is a hiccup?
Burple.

What do you call it when pigs do their laundry?
Hogwash!

What do liars do after they die?
Lie still.

If you crossed King Kong and a bell, what would you have?
A ding-dong King Kong.

How do you know that carrots are good for the eyes?
Have you ever seen a rabbit wearing eyeglasses?

What did the cannibal have for lunch?
Baked beings (beans).

What goes, "Clomp, clomp, clomp, squish. Clomp, clomp, clomp, squish?"

An elephant with a wet sneaker.

Why did the boy's mother knit him three socks for Christmas?

Because he grew another foot.

Why should you stay calm when you meet a cannibal?

You don't want to get into a stew.

What did George Washington say to his men before crossing the Delaware by boat?

"Get in!"

Why was George Washington buried at Mount Vernon?

Because he was dead.

What would you get if Minnehaha married Santa Claus?

Minnehaha hoho.

Where was the Declaration of Independence signed?

At the bottom.

What do you call a knife that cuts four loaves of bread at the same time?

A four-loaf cleaver (clover).

What is white outside, green inside, and hops?

A frog sandwich.

What is a ghoul's favorite food?

Goulash.

What wears a black cape, flies through the night, and bites?

A mosquito in a black cape.

What did the astronaut see on his skillet?

Unidentified frying (flying) objects.

What is a twip?

A twip is what a wabbit takes when he wides a twain.

Why shouldn't you sweep out a room?
The job is too big. Just sweep out the dirt and leave the room there.

Who invented spaghetti?
Someone who used his noodle.

Where do old Volkswagens go?
To the old Volks (folks) home.

What is green and dangerous?
A thundering herd of pickles.

Why do dragons sleep during the day?
So that they can fight knights (nights).

What is yellow, smooth and very dangerous?
Shark-infested custard.

What part of a car causes the most accidents?
The nut behind the wheel.

Why would someone in jail want to catch the measles?
So he could break out.

What would you get if Batman and Robin were run over by a herd of stampeding buffalo?
The Mashed (Masked) Crusaders.

How do you keep a rhinoceros from charging?
Take away his credit cards.

Why is a grouchy kindergarten teacher like a collection of old car parts?

She's a crank surrounded by a bunch of little nuts.

What is a frightened skin diver?

Chicken of the Sea.

What is a fast tricycle?

A tot rod.

What is the best way to hunt bear?

With your clothes off.

What does a mummy child call its parents?

Mummy and Deady.

How do mummies behave?

In a grave manner.

What is on a ghost's bicycle wheels?

Spooks (spokes).

What is a haunted wigwam?

A creepy teepee.

Why did the ghost kid measure himself against the wall?

Because he wanted to know if he gruesome (grew some).

If you cross a dog and an egg, what would you get?

A pooched (poached) egg.

What is a piece of pie in Italian?
A pizza pie.

What do bees do with all their honey?
Cell (sell) it.

What do you get if you cross a clock and a chicken?
An alarm cluck (clock).

What would you get if you crossed a dog and a waffle?
A woofle.

What sound do two porcupines make when they kiss?
"Ouch!"

How do mice kiss?
Mouse-to-mouse (mouth-to-mouth).

How do you stop a dog from barking in the back seat of a car?

Make him sit up front.

What should you do with a blue monster?

Cheer him up.

What is a fat hippie?

A hippo.

If you cross ducks and cows, what would you have?

Quackers (crackers) and milk.

What does a person have to know before teaching tricks to a dog?

More than the dog.

Why did Robin Hood rob the rich?

Because the poor didn't have any money.

Why is an elephant gray, large, and wrinkled?
Because if he were small, white, and round, he would be an aspirin.

What is the difference between an elephant and a jar of peanut butter?
The elephant doesn't stick to the roof of your mouth.

Why did the elephant lie in the middle of the road?
To trip the ants.

What would you get if you crossed a movie house and a swimming pool?
A dive-in theater.

If you found a $10 bill in every pocket of your coat, what would you have?
Someone else's coat.

What did Paul Revere say when he finished his famous ride?
"Whoa!"

Where do they store Chinese boats?
In a junkyard.

What is purple and goes "hmmm?"
An electric grape.

If you need a loan, who do you see in the bank?
The Loan Arranger (Lone Ranger).

What is the difference between Uncle Sam, a rooster, and an old maid who wants to get married?

Uncle Sam says "Yankee Doodle Do," the rooster says "Cock-a-doodle-do," and the old maid says "Any dude'll do!"

What happened when the Scotsman went to buy clothes?

He got kilt (killed).

If an athlete gets athlete's foot, what does an astronaut get?

Missile toe.

How does a snake feel when he sheds his skin?

Snaked.

Which is better to have, a cow or a bull?

A cow gives milk, but a bull always charges.

What happens when a bird flies into a fan?

You get shredded tweet.

If a telegraph operator from California married a telephone operator from Arizona, what would they become?

A western union.

Why is a bride always out of luck on her wedding day?

Because she never marries the best man.

How did the patient get to the hospital so fast?
  Flu.

What did the boy octopus say to the girl octopus?
  "I want to hold your hand, hand, hand, hand, hand, hand, hand, hand."

What should you say when you meet a monster with two heads?
  "Hello, hello!"

What is the best way to talk to a vampire?
  By long distance.

What kind of mistake does a ghost make?
  A boo-boo.

What causes a black eye?
  A guided muscle (missile).

Why did the projector blush?
  It saw the filmstrip.

Why did the traffic light turn red?
*So would you if you had to change in front of all
those people.*

What kind of feet does a mathematics teacher have?
Square feet.

When I get old and ugly, will you still talk to me?
Don't I?

What do you call a sunburn on your stomach?
Pot roast.

What is abcdefghijklmnopqrstuvwxyz, slurp?
Someone eating alphabet soup.

In what kind of home do the buffalo roam?
A very dirty one.

Where does a two-ton gorilla sleep?
Anywhere he wants to.

What is free speech?
When you can use someone else's telephone.

Why is this the last riddle in the book?
Because this is the

END

Index

254

255